THE THOMAS LIGOTTI READER

THE THOMAS LIGOTTI READER

EDITED BY

DARRELL SCHWEITZER

WILDSIDE PRESS

THE THOMAS LIGOTTI READER

To that steadfast literary discoverer, Lee Weinstein.

CONTENTS

INTRODUCTION

This is a book that is probably arriving on time, though it *feels* overdue. It is on time because it takes a while for a substantial body of criticism to develop around a writer. For one thing, the writer has to prove to be other than a flash in the pan. For another, his critics have to develop beyond the initial discovery stage—"Hey! This guy is great!"—into a more considered and thoughtful analysis of the subject's importance and continued development.

But the enthusiast grows impatient. Some of us have been saying, "Hey! This guy is great!" for over twenty years. Indeed, as I write this it has been twenty-one years since Thomas Ligotti's first published story, "The Chymist," appeared in *Nyctalops* #16 (March 1981.) I will admit that I didn't get on the Ligotti "bandwagon" immediately. Like a lot of readers, I more or less ignored the fiction in *Nyctalops*, assuming it to be amateur work, although anyone involved in the small press (as I was) should have known better. But I understood the error of my ways soon enough, as Ligotti continued to develop a "buzz." This was clearly no amateur, beginning writer, but the sort that small presses continuously seek and so seldom find: not a writer who isn't quite good enough for the more commercial markets, but someone who is so genuinely unique, so *weird* in more senses than one, that only the small presses and privately published magazines can accomodate him. That is why small press magazines exist. Arguably Thomas Ligotti justified the existence of the whole horror small-press movement for a generation.

When Harry O. Morris (publisher of *Nyctalops*) issued Ligotti's *Songs of a Dead Dreamer* in a 300 copy edition in 1985, this was a publication which, in retrospect, turned out to be as important (and as collectable) as Lovecraft's *The Shadow Over Innsmouth* (1936)—the first, obscure book by a major talent. But it was only available in an edition of 300 copies. Meanwhile, Ligotti's stories began to make it into a few prestigious anthologies, such as Douglas Winter's *Prime Evil* in 1988. We reprinted a Ligotti story, "The Lost Art of Twilight" in *Weird Tales* in 1990, about the time "The Last Feast of Harlequin" appeared in *The Magazine of Fan-*

tasy & Science Fiction. (So far, amazingly, Ligotti's only appear-ance in *F&SF*.)

I can also reveal now that Weird Tales Library, the book im-print of Terminus Publishing Co., publishers of *Weird Tales*, were planning to issue an expanded version of Ligotti's *Songs of a Dead Dreamer* in the late '80s before history took a different (and, I will admit, more fortunate) course and the new edition of *Songs* be-came the first of four Ligotti volumes to be published by Robinson in England and Carroll & Graf in the United States. These gained their author far more recognition and readership than any small-press edition could have.

The only thing to do at that point was make Ligotti the subject of a special issue of *Weird Tales,* which duly appeared in late 1991. Anyone who hadn't recognized Ligotti's importance by that point had to have been out of touch.

Meanwhile a certain body of Ligotti criticism began to de-velop. A lot of it appeared in a special Ligotti issue of the British magazine *Dagon.* Two articles from that issue are reprinted in this volume. (A third, by Simon McCulloch, exploring "The Lost Art of Twilight," would have been here too, if I had been able to find the author.) S.T. Joshi's piece appeared in the important critical jour-nal, *Studies in Weird Fiction,* which does not often run feature articles about living writers.

And so, by 2003, *The Thomas Ligotti Reader*'s time has come. This book fills an obvious need. If I hadn't compiled it, I am sure someone else would have within a few years. But it is hardly defin-itive. Ligotti is only in mid-career, 49 years of age as this is writ-ten. His fans and afficianados of weird fiction in general can hope that there will be enough material for a second volume before too long.

I was going to repeat the Thomas Ligotti Chronology from my interview book, *Speaking of Horror* at this point, but have decided not to. For one thing, *Speaking of Horror* is in print from Wildside Press. For another, before long I would merely be cribbing from Douglas Anderson's admirably thorough bibliography at the nether end of the book you are holding in your hands. Much bio-graphical information about Ligotti is to be found in the interviews I've reprinted.

So here are a few basic facts:

1953. Thomas Ligotti born in Detroit, Michigan.

1971. Graduates from Grosse Pointe North High School.

1975. Receives B.A. degree in English from Wayne State University (Detroit).

1979. Joins Literary Criticism Division of the Gale Research Company, and continues to work there until moving to Florida in 2001.

1981. First published story, "The Chymist," in *Nyctalops* #16 (March).

And so on. The Thomas Ligotti story is far from over.

—Darrell Schweitzer
Philadelphia, Pennsylvania

THOMAS LIGOTTI'S CAREER OF NIGHTMARES

Matt Cardin

Thomas Ligotti is arguably the preëminent living writer of horror fiction. This reputation has grown up around him over a period of twenty years, during which time he has remained paradoxically obscure in the mainstream literary consciousness, and even, astonishingly, among some segments of horror fandom. Probably more people are acquainted with him unawares through his editorial work for The Gale Group (the famous academic publishing company, for which he worked for over twenty years) than are acquainted with his stories. Nevertheless, he has produced a substantial body of fiction that has generated a passionately devoted fan base, and his work has been soundly praised by critics and readers alike. Reviewers have written glowingly of his books, and his publisher has mined these reviews for blurbs. (From *The New York Review of Science Fiction*: "Ligotti is probably the genre's most committed purist. He perfectly expresses the 'disorienting strangeness' that is the hallmark of the weird;" from *The New York Times Book Review*: "If there were a literary genre called 'philosophical horror,' Thomas Ligotti's *[Grimscribe]* would easily fit within it . . . provocative images and a style that is both entertaining and lyrical;" From *The Philadelphia Inquirer*: "Thomas Ligotti has had one of the most quietly extraordinary careers in the history of horror fiction;" From *The Washington Post*: "Thomas Ligotti is the best kept secret in contemporary horror fiction . . . the best new American writer of weird fiction to appear in years;" From *Interzone*: "Ligotti is wonderful and original; he has a dark vision of a new and special kind, a vision that no one had before him."). His admirers are wont to call him the best author the horror genre has ever produced, and while such sweeping statements are always questionable at best, it has become increasingly difficult to deny at least the possible validity of the claim. At a bare minimum, it seems undeniable that Ligotti has secured for himself a unique and lasting position of importance in the world of horror fiction, and probably in the wider world of literature in general.

His career as a professional horror author dates back to the early 1980s, when his stories first began appearing in such small press mainstays as *Nyctalops, Grimoire, Eldritch Tales, Fantasy Macabre,* and *Dark Horizons.* These stories spoke with a shockingly distinct voice, and their subject matter was, to say the least, unique. For example, "The Chymist," first published in 1981 in *Nyctalops* vol. III, no. 2, speculates about the cosmic forces underlying the world of matter itself—"The Great Chemists," as the narrator calls them—and offers a glimpse of what happens when these forces decide to "dream" an individual into new and nightmarish shapes. "Dream of a Mannikin," first published in 1982 in *Eldritch Tales* vol. 2, no. 3, offers a horrific take on the eastern philosophical idea of multileveled selfhood. "Dr. Voke and Mr. Veech," first published in 1983 in *Grimoire* no. 5, poses disturbing questions about the nature and possible consciousness of puppets, dolls, mannikins, and other effigies of the human form, and also about the relationship of these effigies to their makers and manipulators. "Notes on the Writing of Horror: A Story," first published in 1985 in *Dark Horizons* no. 28, offers exactly what the first part of the title would seem to indicate: a series of notes on how to write horror stories. But then the narrative pulls an ingenious roundabout on the reader by revealing that the narrator is not as safely removed from the subject matter of his notes as he has led himself and his reader to believe.

The profoundly dark philosophical slant of these early stories had the inevitable effect of creating a cult following for Ligotti. His outlook was despairing, even nihilistic, and this proved to be a point of contact with many readers who, while they may not have explicitly shared his outlook, still found within themselves a resonance of the black truths about which he so powerfully wrote. Quite a few such readers had the unsettling (and somehow exhilarating) impression that Ligotti was expressing in his stories their own deepest, darkest insights.

He also brought to his stories a distinctive literary style to match the distinctiveness of his themes. In his own words, he was for a time a "fanatical student of literary styles, the more bizarre and artificial the better."[1] An example of this stylistic obsession can be seen in the fact that when he conceived the maniacal narrative voice of most of his early stories, he was consciously emulating the style of Russian-born writer Vladimir Nabakov.[2] In spite of this imitation—or perhaps because of it—his stories were in the end wholly original. When his first book of collected stories, *Songs of a Dead Dreamer,* was published in a mass market edition in 1989 (having been published three years earlier in a limited small-press edition), readers encountered no less a genre heavyweight than Ramsey Campbell saying in the introduction, "Despite faint echoes of writers he admires . . . Ligotti's vision is wholly personal. Few other writers could conceive a horror story in the form of notes on the writing of the genre, and I can't think of any other writer who could have brought it off."

In the same introduction, Campbell wrote that the book "has to be one of the most important horror books of the decade," and with these words the proverbial cat was let out of the allegorical bag. Ligotti's readership still remained relatively small compared to the Kings and Koontz's of the world (as should have been expected, considering that his fiction was highly literary and idiosyncratic, and was most certainly not written for a mass audience), but his early reputation as the reigning dark magus of the horror world began to precede him, and more and more genre fans began to realize that this was a writer they simply had to read. In one of the more bizarre and amusing incidents of his literary career, Ligotti's innate reclusiveness, combined with the mysterious reputation he had gained from his fiction, gave rise to the rumor that he did not really exist but was instead a pseudonym for some more famous author. When Poppy Z Brite asked in her introduction to Ligotti's 1996 omnibus collection *The Nightmare Factory,* "Are you out there, Thomas Ligotti?" she echoed thousands of readers who were asking the same question, readers who wondered what the man was really like, or whether he even existed.

At the time of this writing (April 2000), Ligotti has five more collections of stories to his credit after *Songs of a Dead Dreamer.* In chronological order, these are *Grimscribe: His Lives and Works* (1991), *Noctuary* (1994), *The Agonizing Resurrection of Victor Frankenstein and Other Gothic Tales* (1994), *The Nightmare Fac-*

tory (1996), and *In a Foreign Town, In a Foreign Land* (1997). This last book was written in conjunction with the experimental music group Current93, and was released with an accompanying CD of music supplement the book. (Since the exact relationship of the book and CD have never been specified, it is also theoretically possible to view the former as supplementing the latter.) Ligotti's story "The Nightmare Network" was published in editor John Pelan's 1996 anthology *Darkside: Horror for the Next Millennium*, and in late 1999 Ligotti gained his widest exposure yet when his story "The Shadow, The Darkness" was published in editor Al Sarrantonio's high-profile anthology *999: New Tales of Horror and Suspense* alongside works by such genre icons as Stephen King, Peter Straub, and William Peter Blatty. In February of 2000, Current93 released a CD titled *I Have a Special Plan for This World* in which the narrated text was written entirely by Ligotti.[3]

For the uninitiated who are thinking of delving into Ligotti's work, or for those who have not yet made up their mind, or even for those who have read some of his work and are wondering where to go next, there are a number of pertinent factors to consider. Firstly, it should be mentioned that Ligotti has repeatedly cited Lovecraft and Poe as being the two most important influences on his life and work, respectively, and many fans of these authors have discovered in Ligotti a kindred spirit. In particular, the Lovecraft connection has continued to bring Ligotti a steady stream of new readers. He is very open about the fact that it was Lovecraft who originally inspired him to try his hand at fiction, and although he has said that Lovecraft's influence on him is more personal than literary, most readers find a very strong Lovecraftian element in many of Ligotti's stories. An example of direct Lovecraftian influence can be found in *Grimscribe* in "The Last Feast of Harlequin," which is the earliest-written of Ligotti's stories, and which is dedicated "To the memory of H.P. Lovecraft." Another direct influence can be found in *Songs of a Dead Dreamer* in the story titled "The Sect of the Idiot," where Ligotti mentions Lovecraft's infamous tome of black magic, the *Necronomicon*, and also makes reference to Lovecraft's "blind idiot god" Azathoth. Perhaps the most important and pervasive Lovecraftian influence in

Ligotti's fiction is found in his repeatedly reworked idea of a mystical, ontologically absolute evil—in e.g. "Dream of a Mannikin," "Masquerade of a Dead Sword," "Nethescurial," "The Tsalal," "The Shadow, The Darkness"—which bears at times a similarity to Lovecraft's mythology of certain monstrous extracosmic entities or forces that continually impinge upon the little world of human interests and emotions. While there are significant divergences between the two men's literary styles and personal visions, many Lovecraft fans have felt that, in a way, Ligotti "takes up" where Lovecraft left off—that is, that Ligotti is saying what Lovecraft might have said if he were alive today—and it may not be too far off the mark to consider the bulk of Ligotti's fiction as a kind of distillation and expression in contemporary terms of what was best in Lovecraft. In short, those who appreciate Lovecraft will almost certainly find something to appreciate in Ligotti.

Secondly, when approaching any writer for the first time, there is always the question of which book or books one ought to read first. Fortunately, in Ligotti's case the answer is obvious. The *Nightmare Factory,* as mentioned above, is an omnibus of his work, reprinting most of the stories from the previous collections (with the exception of *Agonizing Resurrection*) and adding to them six new stories in a section titled "Teatro Grottesco and Other Tales." As such, it forms an ideal introduction to his work. The only drawback is that some of his best and most cherished stories from past collections have been omitted. Gone are his two metafictional explorations from *Songs of a Dead Dreamer,* "Notes on the Writing of Horror" and "Professor Nobody's Little Lectures on Supernatural Horror." Gone also is the entire final section of *Noctuary,* titled "Notebook of the Night" and consisting of a series of nineteen prose poems or vignettes which in the opinion of this author represent some of Ligotti's most powerful work. Not even mentioned is the wonderful *The Agonizing Resurrection of Victor Frankenstein and Other Gothic Tales,* which consists of a series of vignette-length reworkings of classic literary and cinematic horror tales, and which may in fact be Ligotti's best book when measured against his other books purely in terms of their overall success as collections. Having said this, *The Nightmare Factory* is still the single best book for the Ligotti neophyte to purchase. It presents a

sweeping overview of his perennial thematic and stylistic obsessions, and the new stories in "Teatro Grottesco and Other Tales"
represent him at the height of his powers. The book also contains a
valuable introductory essay by Ligotti titled "The Consolations of
Horror," in which he considers the question of why readers read
and writers write such things, and why it is that horror, "at least
in its artistic representations, can be a comfort." He considers and
rejects several alternative answers to this question, arriving finally at the conclusion that artistic horror offers only a single valid
consolation: "simply that someone shares some of your own
feelings and has made of these a work of art which you have the
insight, sensitivity, and—like it or not—peculiar set of experiences
to appreciate."

A final consideration that ought to be borne in mind by the
prospective reader is that Ligotti's stories tend to have a profound
emotional impact. His vision is exceedingly dark, and it is possible
for his stories to infect the reader with a mild-to-severe case of depression. It is even possible for them to effect a change in the
reader's self-perception and view of the universe. This warning is
not meant to be sensationalistic, nor is it meant to turn new readers away. It is simply a statement of fact based upon the experiences of actual readers. Ligotti writes about the darkest of themes
with an amazing power, and he means what he says. Often his stories seem to communicate a message below their surface, a sort of
subliminal statement that should not rightly be able to traverse
the barrier of verbal language. This has not gone unnoticed by his
fans and peers in the horror industry. For example, Brian
McNaughton, winner of the 1998 World Fantasy Award for his collection of stories *The Throne of Bones,* dedicated his story "ystery
orm" to Ligotti, and in the story (which can be found in Pelan's
Darkside anthology) he describes Ligotti's literary power thusly:

> To translate dreams into plain prose, into the bald speech of
> post-literate America, seemed impossible until he read the tales of
> Edward F. Tourmalign [a fictionalized Ligotti]. In Tourmalign's
> stories, wind-blown leaflets, clinking light-stanchions in empty
> streets, neon signs with missing letters—such banal images as-
> sumed, in waking life and in cold print, the horrific significance
> they so often radiated in nightmares. It had been said of many

pathetic hacks that they should never be read at night, but it made no difference when one read Tourmalign, for his work was a poison that infiltrated the bloodstream and changed the structure of the brain.

To illustrate the point from one of Ligotti's own works, let the reader consider the following long passage from "The Shadow at the Bottom of the World," in which the communal narrator of an unspecified rural town experiences strange dreams during an unnatural prolongation of the autumn season:

In sleep we were consumed by the feverish life of the earth, cast among a ripe, fairly rotting world of strange growth and transformation. We took a place within a darkly flourishing landscape where even the air was ripened into ruddy hues and everything wore the wrinkled grimace of decay, the mottled complexion of old flesh. The face of the land itself was knotted with so many other faces, ones that were corrupted by vile impulses. Grotesque expressions were molding themselves into the darkish grooves of ancient bark and the whorls of withered leaf; pulpy, misshapen features peered out of damp furrows; and the crisp skin of stalks and dead seeds split into a multitude of crooked smiles. All was a freakish mask painted with russet, rashy colors—colors that bled with a virulent intensity, so rich and vibrant that things trembled with their own ripeness. But despite this gross palpability, there remained something spectral at the heart of these dreams. It moved in shadow, a presence that was in the world of solid forms but not of it. Nor did it belong to any other world that could be named, unless it was to that realm which is suggested to us by an autumn night when fields lay ragged in moonlight and some wild spirit has entered into things, a great aberration sprouting forth from a chasm of moist and fertile shadows, a hollow-eyed howling malignity rising to present itself to the cold emptiness of space and the pale gaze of the moon.

In this passage one can clearly feel Ligotti's magic at work. His careful choices of rhythm, sound, and vocabulary work synergistically to produce an oneiric effect, so that the "fairly rotting world of faint growth and transformation" which hints at a spectral presence that is a "great aberration sprouting forth from a chasm of moist and fertile shadows" becomes identified in the reader's mind with the world of dreams and nightmares. Here and elsewhere, Ligotti is remarkably successful in his attempt at using language to convey this most elusive of moods .

On a more philosophical note, we can discern three primary themes (although they are certainly not the only three) emerging from a survey of Ligotti's *oeuvre*: first, the meaninglessness—or possibly malevolence—of the reality principle behind the material universe; second, the perennial instability of this universe of solid forms, shapes, and concepts as it threatens to collapse or mutate into something monstrous and unforeseeable; and third, the nightmarishness of conscious personal existence in such a world. The stories in the "Teatro Grottesco" section of *The Nightmare Factory* provide a good example of these themes at work. In many ways these stories are the most personal of Ligotti's works, and as such they provide the literary equivalent of an intravenous dose of his mood. "The Bungalow House" is especially notable in this regard, for in it the narrator states what might be taken for a Ligottian philosophical and artistic credo, if such a thing were possible. Upon discovering a series of performance art audio tapes in the form of "dream monologues," the narrator is surprised and gratified, and also somewhat disturbed, to discover that another person shares his own love for "the icy bleakness of things." He reflects:

> I wanted to believe that this artist had escaped the dreams and demons of all sentiment in order to explore the foul and crummy delights of a universe where everything had been reduced to three stark principles: first, that there was nowhere for you to go; second, that there was nothing for you to do; and third, that there was no one for you to know. Of course, I knew that this view was an illusion like any other, but it was also one that had sustained me so long and so well—as long and as well as any other illusion and perhaps longer, perhaps better.

This passage recalls Nietzsche's assertion in *The Birth of Tragedy* that "It is only as an aesthetic phenomenon that existence and the world are eternally justified." In a universe reduced to those "three stark principles," the only pleasures one can safely enjoy—that is, the only pleasures one can enjoy without the threat of disappointment and painful disillusionment—are purely aesthetic. At the same time, the narrator is aware that this attitude is itself an illusion, and that he holds to it merely out of its proven utility. But ultimately even this painfully worked out maze of psychic defenses is not enough to shield him from utter despair. After a series of disturbing events, he finds himself unable to take any more pleasure from the works of this new artist, and is left only with a desperate need to find release from "this heartbreaking sadness I suffer every minute of the day (and night), this killing sadness that feels as if it will never leave me no matter where I go or what I do or whom I may ever know."

This idea is foundational to Ligotti's fictional universe: there is simply no solace to be found anywhere in this or any other world. Nor is this merely a literary affectation; Ligotti is using the vehicle of horror fiction to express his actual experience of life. When questioned by one interviewer about the relationship between his writing and his personal outlook on life, he replied, "My outlook is that it's a damn shame that organic life ever developed on this or any other planet, and that the pain that living creatures necessarily suffer makes for an existence that is a perennial nightmare. This attitude underlies almost everything I've written."[4] The close connection between his personal outlook and his stories holds true for even his most extravagant fictional creations. In "Nethescurial," for example, he writes of an ancient pantheistic religious cult whose members discovered at some point in prehistory that their deity was evil, and that their religion was in truth a sort of "pandemonism." As commentary to this idea, Ligotti has said,

> It seems to me that living beings on this planet suffer at the hands of an insatiable and wildly creative force-which has variously been referred to as Anima Mundi, Elan Vital, the Will (Schopenhauer) that does not have our interests at heart, or the interests of any particular species for that matter, since it has extinguished more forms of life than it has created. From the point of view of individuals existing in this luxuriant world, this force must necessarily be viewed as inimical to our comfort and sanity, although almost no one holds to this attitude.[5]

In the end, it is this direct connection between Ligotti's personal outlook and his fictional world that lends his writing such power. His technical literary skills are truly marvelous, but without the strength of his vision to empower them, they would amount to nothing more than a literary sound and light show. He has devoted himself to a career of nightmares, a career of expressing in literary form the demons that have afflicted him for most of his adult life. In interviews he has spoken candidly of his own "erstwhile craving for 'enlightenment in darkness',"[6] and the fruit of this craving can be seen in the fact that through his fiction he provides an aesthetic approximation of this very enlightenment for his readers. Christine Morris, writing in *Dagon* 22/23, said, "Receptive reader, be forewarned—if you read for more than escapist entertainment, if you read to be challenged or enlightened, if you read to explore not only daydreams but nightmares, Thomas Ligotti's stories may transform you, too."[7] For those readers who already possess "the insight, sensitivity, and—like it or not—peculiar set of experiences" to appreciate Ligotti's vision, this transformation may already be well underway even before they encounter the master's books. In true Ligottian fashion, perhaps his stories will always speak most vividly to those rare persons in whom the seed of darkness has already been sown. In their own half-conscious pilgrimage toward a dark enlightenment, these sensitive seekers will follow Ligotti willingly into the depths of the nightmare, and there in the echoing stillness of the silent, staring void they will find that they are looking into the radiant black reflection of their own shadowed souls.

NOTES:

1. Robert Bee. "Interview with Thomas Ligotti." 1999. Thomas Ligotti Online. http://www. longshadows.com/ligotti/bee.html (4/05/00).

2. R.F. Paul and Keith Schurholz. "Triangulating the Daemon: an Interview with Thomas Ligotti." *Esoterra* 8 (Winter/Spring 1999): 17.

3. For the only complete bibliography of Ligotti's work, see "Thomas Ligotti: a Bibliography," compiled and edited by Douglas Anderson, at Thomas Ligotti Online at http://www.longshadows.com/ligotti/biblio.html.

4. Bee, "Interview with Thomas Ligotti," op. cit.

5. See the mini-interview with Ligotti in the commentary on "Nethescurial" at Thomas Ligotti Online (http://www.longshadows.com/ligotti/ss-ne.html).

6. Bee, "Interview with Thomas Ligotti," op. cit.

7. Christine Morris. "Beyond Dualism: An Appreciation of the Writings of Thomas Ligotti." *Dagon* 22/23 (September-December 1988): 12.

WORKS CITED:

Anderson, Douglas, compiler and editor. "Thomas Ligotti: A Bibliography." 2000. Thomas Ligotti Online (http://www.longshadows.com/ligotti/biblio.html).

Bee, Robert. "Interview with Thomas Ligotti." 1999. Thomas Ligotti Online. http://www. longshadows.com/ligotti/bee.html (4/05/00).

Cardin, Matt. Commentary on "Nethescurial" at Thomas Ligotti Online (http://www.longshadows.com/ligotti/ss-ne.html).

Morris, Christine. "Beyond Dualism: An Appreciation of the Writings of Thomas Ligotti." *Dagon* 22/23 (September-December 1988): 10-12.

Paul, R.F. and Keith Schurholz. "Triangulating the Daemon: an Interview with Thomas Ligotti." *Esoterra* 8 (Winter/Spring 1999): 14-21.

WEIRD TALES TALKS WITH THOMAS LIGOTTI

Darrell Schweitzer

Schweitzer: Tom, your career has followed quite a different trajectory from that of most writers. You have achieved considerable prominence *without* the traditional reliance on novels, or even publication in many major outlets. You seem to be one of the very few writers to become genuinely famous through the small press. Then you jump from special Ligotti issues of *Crypt of Cthulhu* and *Dagon* to having your collection, *Songs of a Dead Dreamer*, published by a mainstream house, Carroll & Graf. I'm impressed, and so, I am sure, are quite a lot of other people. What's your secret?

Thomas Ligotti: I don't see my situation as unprecedented by any means, especially when you consider the case of someone like T.E.D. Klein, who became a major "presence" in weird fiction-land after the publication of only a few stories. Or Ramsey Campbell, who could have dropped dead after publishing *Demons By Daylight* and still loomed large in the post-Lovecraft era of supernatural horror writing.

Maybe my perspective is a bit insular, but I find it difficult to imagine myself as approaching the stature of early Klein or Campbell, and in any case psychologically unprofitable to do so. Nevertheless, I do feel fortunate in gaining the attention of some hard-core fanatics of horror tales, from Harry O. Morris, who illustrated and published the original, limited-run, Silver Scarab Press edition of *Songs of a Dead Dreamer*, to editors and writers like Douglas Winter, Robert Price, Ramsey Campbell, Stefan Dziemianowicz, Michael Ashley, and some guy named Darrell Schweitzer.

Schweitzer: Then where do you fit into the context of weird literature, or literature in general, both as a writer and as a reader?

Ligotti: For my part, I suppose that I managed to find a certain audience in readers who still take seriously, as I do, writers like

Poe and Lovecraft as well as a great many other writers whose works are related to the supernatural genre without being strictly demarcated by its conventions. This latter group forms a gallery of eccentric, for the most part grim-minded and occasionally demented figures in world literature, from Aloysius Bertrand to the late 19th century decadents to early 20th century writers like Georg Trakl and Bruno Schulz and more recent masters of the post-modern nightmare, including Samuel Beckett, Dino Buzzati, and Jorge Luis Borges.

In general, my reading tends toward authors of a morbid, negative type. These are really the ones who have perpetuated the tradition of horror in literature, because their works reveal the outrageously strange and terrible as integral to existence, a fascinating turbulence never to be quelled, and not simply a momentary or isolated aberration succeeded by reconciliation with the world, or even its affirmation. Lately I've been reading the melancholy aphorisms of Logan Pearsall Smith and the novels, which are more properly described as multi-hundred page monologues, of Thomas Bernhard.

Schweitzer: What got you started writing and when?

Ligotti: I started writing—outside of school assignments, that is—about my third year of college. I found the required writing that I was doing to be very stimulating: it made me high, or at least distracted me from my chronic anxiety, and I wanted to do more of it. This was very like the experience I had with reading—I had read only a few books before college—only more intense. I was very much aware that for me both reading and writing were practiced as a form of escapism, but in a paradoxical way since I usually escaped *into* a sort of imaginary hell. Perhaps you might call this a *confrontational* escapism.

Schweitzer: For all your success, you can't possibly be earning a living from short stories and a single collection, no matter how prestigiously it may be published. So, what else do you do?

Ligotti: I've earned my living for the past fourteen years doing editorial work for a reference book company in Detroit called Gale Research. I work in the literary criticism division of the company, which produces several series of books that reprint selected commentary on authors from antiquity to the present day. Many, if not most of the entries we compile represent the first, and probably only, time that anyone has gathered English-language criticism on that author. Where else can you find an assemblage of critical writings on the works of Hans Heinz Ewers, not to mention a picture of the scarred mug of horror literature's favorite Nazi apologist?

Schweitzer: Let's talk about the influence of Lovecraft on your work. It's virtually impossible to come into this field without falling under the shadow of H.P.L. at some point, and I should think it would be completely impossible to do so in the pages of *Nyctalops,* which is where many readers first encountered you. Yet your stories only resemble Lovecraft's in the most tenuous manner, in that you too seem to depict a bleak and uncertain universe in which human assumptions don't apply very far. But the more overt Lovecraftisms, from the adjectives to the tentacular Things From Beyond, are conspicuously absent.

Ligotti: I think your characterization of Lovecraft's literary universe as "bleak and uncertain" is accurate enough, especially with respect to works like "The Music of Erich Zann" and "The Colour Out of Space." The more science-fictiony stories like "At the Mountains of Madness" and "The Shadow Out of Time" are arguably another matter, since they outline metaphysical schemes that are not at all uncertain, perhaps even too simplistic and comprehensible, and certainly depict a universe that is no less "grand" and no more bleak than those of most religious and myth systems. What is missing in Lovecraft are the human relationships that serve as the focus and prime impetus of almost all fiction, horror and otherwise. While such relationships may serve as either a source of fear or a safety net, the bottom line is that they divert attention from the macrocosmic mysteries which may be exalting or dreadful or both, depending on one's mood; but these cosmic mysteries never offer the kind of hope and potential consolation that lurks behind the pages of practically all horror fiction since its beginnings in the gothic novel. So, yes, I would agree that my stories could be called

Lovecraftian in having a fairly steady view of the bleak and uncertain cosmos.

Schweitzer: You seem to differ from Lovecraft in your lack of scientific realism. Remember how H.P.L. used to say that a story should be put together with all the care of a thorough-going hoax? Yours seem to be more like disturbing dreams. I don't see the realist-hoaxer in you. So, is this a partial rejection of the Lovecraftian method, or just a difference in sensibilities?

Ligotti: As far as Lovecraft's fictional method of "scientific realism" is concerned, I can't believe that Lovecraft ever looked back on any of his works and considered them to be successful realism, though at certain points in his career there were stories partly based on the Poe-instigated intention of pulling off a literary hoax, a strategy Poe himself almost never employed in his horror tales.

Lovecraft always veered off into a highly unrealistic, as well as highly poetic style. He was at his worst when he tried to be "convincing" in the manner derived from the late 19th century realist-naturalist writers. And of course toward the end of his life Lovecraft expressed in his letters quite a bit of confusion concerning the most effective approach to weird fiction, feeling that with few exceptions he had failed to capture in literary form his most powerful sensations and visions. It's no news that he always feared that his exposure to the stories in *Weird Tales* would pervert his ideals and methods as a horror writer, and to an extent this fear seems to have been realized.

Schweitzer: What do you think a good horror story should be? Should it raise shrieks, or is disquiet enough?

Ligotti: I can only attempt an answer by stating my biases regarding what a horror story should *not* be. This is very risky, because there are so many impurities in any form of literature, and in fact the essential interest of literature itself may well depend on the impure concoction of the artistic use of language and the human experience that for the most part motivates literary language. If literature as a whole is largely founded on impurity, how can any specialized form such as the horror tale aspire to purity, especially when so many of the impurities are the result of an often quite interesting cross-pollination with other literary forms? It can't, of course; it can only fight the same losing battle of every other human endeavor. This battle, most of all, is against the popular *pull* of the horror genre. As Poe rightly declared, "Terror is not of Germany"—or the United States—"but of the soul." And while that soul may be strolling down the streets of San Francisco or the sidewalks of New York, it ultimately paces in isolation in a realm all its own, a realm that is as claustrophobic as a nightmare and as expansive as . . . well, you get the idea. No doubt any form of writing is popular within a certain circle, but if that circle is too wide it remains one-dimensional, lying flat on the earth rather than spinning into a sphere that moves through stranger dimensions.

Schweitzer: I don't really understand what you mean by the "impure concoction of the artistic use of language and the human experience that motivates literary language" and forms the essential interest of literature. Do you mean that if somehow we were able to write with absolute and utter clarity and understand the impulses and experiences that went into the writing just as absolutely and clearly, there would be no fruitful ambiguity left and therefore no further basis for literature?

Ligotti: I probably over-expressed myself. Very simply, I'm referring to the possibility that the fascination of reading may derive neither from the subject portrayed nor from the language that portrays it but from the relationship between the two—that is, a relationship in which literary language does not communicate subject matter but rather *processes* it, a debased intercourse between life and art, the offspring of which is a recombined creature born of experience and expression. A unique little bastard.

Schweitzer: To put it another way then, what do you most admire about the stories you do admire?

Ligotti: The technique of delineating a condition of pervasive strangeness and unease is the approach I most admire in horror fiction, and the one that supports the haunting memorableness of such tales as Algernon Blackwood's "The Willows" and

Lovecraft's "The Colour Out of Space." Like electroshock therapy, sudden or violent frights of the "pop-up" type may make a strong momentary impression, but overall the effect is to annihilate the emotion and the consciousness that are crucial for a really profound sense of horror, the purest possible sense of horror.

Schweitzer: You also write horror fiction *about* horror fiction. Surely that is a delicate act to pull off. What are the strengths and limitations of this approach?

Ligotti: The nature of horror fiction is a subject like any other, though one that probably interests a relatively small faction of the horror-reading public. Then again, the one knowable trait shared by all readers of horror fiction is that they read horror fiction, so why shouldn't they be interested? I imagine that most readers, whatever their taste in fiction, end up reading the same basic story told in the same basic style until the day they die.

Schweitzer: The *pull* of horror literature, as I see it, is not toward self-examination of the form, but in the direction of the Stephen King or Dean Koontz type of story, which is easily understood and completely within the reader's frame of everyday reference, *and* very emotionally compelling. In other words, make 'em laugh, make 'em cry, rip their hearts out, but make sure you do it in Suburbia, U.S.A. 1991. My guess is that King has such wide appeal not so much for his monsters as for his ability to depict fathers and sons (and husbands and wives) drawn together by crisis. Common emotions, honestly and clearly presented. That's the way to multi-millionaire superstardom.

Ligotti: Your analysis could be extended to best-selling fiction in general. The works that enjoy the most success in the marketplace are naturally those that are the most accessible to the greatest number of people. Hence, Beckett's big hit is *Waiting for Godot*, which is relatively easy to *get* when contrasted with just about any of his other works. Poe is most celebrated for his detective stories and holds an honored place in that genre, but to contemporary readers of horror fiction he's practically invisible, judging from the minimal attention his works receive in horrorzines and the infrequency with which his name arises in interviews with horror writers of today. Why should this be the case? Because his horror stories, when placed beside his detective stories, are poetic and obscure. Most readers have little patience or sympathy with such works. This is perfectly understandable. I'm very much this way when it comes to movies. With few exceptions, I don't care for artistically ambitious, serious films and can only tolerate action extravaganzas or adaptations of blockbuster horror novels.

Schweitzer: How about something more about yourself? Did you have an upbringing which directed you toward writing horror fiction?

Ligotti: Almost certainly, but it's difficult to say just how. For instance, when I was two years old I was operated on for an internal rupture. Now, Bram Stoker also underwent surgery as an infant and there's an article that asserts the effect of this early "surgical trauma" on his writings. I'm told that I was quite alert and cheerful throughout this ordeal, including the truss-wearing aftermath, but I've noticed in the last couple of years that a disproportionate number of my tales feature doctors of one sort or another. But who really knows?

Another for-instance: I was a Catholic until I was eighteen years old, when I unloaded all of the doctrines, but almost none of the fearful superstition, of a gothically devout childhood and youth. This superstitiousness was abetted in a small way by an old woman who used to babysit me and my two younger brothers. Her name was Mrs. Rinaldi and she specialized in telling religious cautionary tales. One of them particularly impressed me. It was about a poor woman who kept finding her laundry pulled from the clothesline outside her house and trampled in the dirt. She thought the Devil was doing this deed when actually it was just the neighborhood kids. In her irrational state of exasperation, she offered to give the Devil anything if he would allow her a clean batch of clothes. Well, the Devil takes care of the pranksters, all right, and then demands the woman fulfill her part of the bargain by turning over to him her infant son, which she has no choice but to do. Years later the son, who is now a full-grown demon, pays a visit to his mother to show her what she has done to him. There's something very captivating about this atrociously senseless tale. I was reminded of it recently in reading a collection of Eskimo folktales. What nightmares those people dreamed up! *Very* nice.

Probably the most important factor in my taking interest in writing fiction in general was the emotional breakdown I alluded to earlier. This occurred in August 1970, following intense use of drugs and booze, though these intoxicants served only as a catalyst for a fate that my high-strung and mood-swinging self would have encountered at some point. Before that time, I had no interest in reading or writing, though I tested well in these subjects; afterward, they became the only ways I could alter my state of mind without fear, at least without *extreme* fear, of losing my grip entirely. My condition is called agoraphobia; it's part hereditary, and I continue to experience its symptoms, including panic attacks and a general sense of unreality.

Schweitzer: Did you ever have any other plans for your life, other than to be a writer?

Ligotti: No. Having an identity as a horror writer is about the closest thing I've come to distinctly *doing* anything with my life. When I was a kid I had a vague ambition to be a baseball player, then a rock-and-roll musician. I still fool around with electric guitar privately, but there's not much to be said for my musical ability. Recreationally, I also attend the local harness-race tracks regularly with my younger brother, who introduced me to the manic-depressive pleasures of this pastime and who is the dedicatee of my second collection of horror stories. You want to know terror? Try waiting for the results of a photo-finish between the horse you loaded up on and some other hay-burner.

Schweitzer: What are you working on for the near future? While we're at it, do you have any thoughts on where your future is as a horror writer?

Ligotti: It's hard to say. I'd like to write more than I have in the past few years, but I'm often too distracted or lack the energy to do anything about it. This is probably just as well.

Schweitzer: Thanks, Tom.

THE MYSTAGOGUE, THE GNOSTIC QUEST, THE SECRET BOOK

Robert M. Price

Virtually all of the fiction of Thomas Ligotti enshrines and presupposes a very definite worldview. As Ligotti's Professor Nobody makes clear to us, his students, the "logic of supernatural horror . . . is a logic that is founded on fear; it is a logic whose sole principle states: 'Existence equals Nightmare.' Unless life is a dream, nothing makes sense." ("Professor Nobody's Little Lectures on Supernatural Horror," *Songs of a Dead Dreamer*, p. 145) [1]. In "The Sect of the Idiot," this mad worldview is identified with H. P.Lovecraft's: all is idiot chaos. It is possible in Ligotti's universe to attain a revelatory glimpse of this final truth of insanity, a "terrible enlightenment . . . revealing an intolerable knowledge, some ultimate disclosure concerning the order of things" ("The Sect of the Idiot,"*Crypt of Cthulhu* #56, p.13). And those who have shared this vision, its prophets, seem always in Ligotti's tales to find themselves incarcerated in the madhouse, as do Victor Keirion ("Vastarien") and John Doe ("The Frolic"). "Dr. Locrian's Asylum" actually functions as an occult research laboratory because the voices of the inmates "speak the supreme delirium of the planets . . . dancing in the blackness. In the wandering words of those lunatics . . . the ancient mysteries are restored." (*Grue* #5, p.83). Here Ligotti sounds almost like psychologist R. D. Laing.

If the so-called madmen are the ones who perceive the truth of the Ligottian cosmos, what does this bode for the legions of the conventionally sane? Just that: we proclaim ourselves sane by mere shared convention, shared delusion. The monologue of Klaus Klingman in "The Mystics of Muelenberg" reveals that without the constant effort of us all to "stick to the common story," the world as we "know" it would rapidly begin to blur and dissolve, and in the rare moment of weariness we may be caught off guard and "let down our burden" of what sociologists-of-knowledge Berger and Luckmann have called "cognitive world maintenance" (Peter Berger and Thomas Luckmann, *The Social Construction of Real-*

ity, 1966/67). "This a Ligotti character calls "a hallucinatory view of creation" ("The Mystics of Muelenberg," p.32). What is envisioned here might be called a version of George Berkeley's epistemology of Immaterialism without its lynchpin, God. To the old question whether a tree falling in a deserted forest makes noise, Berkeley answered yes because the omniscient God sees all. In Ligotti's world, there is no such guarantee, so we have to keep careful watch or we will disabuse ourselves of "the myth of the natural universe—that is, one that adheres to certain continuities whether we wish them or not." ("The Mystics of Muelenberg," p.32)

A similar image is that of group hypnosis. In "The Sect of the Idiot" the insect-like Norns of Azathoth (my terminology) keep the "world in a trance; a hypnotized parade of beings sleep-walking to the odious manipulations of their whispering masters, those hooded freaks *who were themselves among the hypnotized." (Crypt of Cthulhu* #56, p.14). A small scale example of the same phenomena, a microcosm if you will, is provided by the hypnotist of "Drink to Me Only with Labyrinthine Eyes" whose spell keeps the whole crowd under the illusion of beauty until they are rudely awakened to what has all the while been the true horror of the situation. In this tale, which recalls at once "The Emperor's New Clothes," and Lovecraft's "The Outsider," we are tempted to see a picture of Ligotti himself and his literary mission: to spin a web of enchantment carrying his audience to the final realization of the horror of all existence.

Closely related to the hypnosis theme is that of puppetry. Ligotti frequently compares characters to mere puppets, especially in "Dream of a Mannikin" and "Dr. Voke and Mr. Veech."

Ligotti's work, and his picture of reality, must also be understood against the background of the Decadent movement. The final desirable, beautiful, and true is "that summit or abyss of the unreal, that paradise of exhaustion, confusion, and debris where reality ends and where one may dwell among its ruins" ("Vastarien," *Crypt of Cthulhu* #48, p.25). Strictly speaking, the glory of decadence in view here is not the decay of reality on its own perceived level, but rather the decay, collapse, or ruination of that very level of perception.

For the hypnotized herd of everyday perceivers, stark fear of the truth makes them fortify the illusion, but for a few seekers "the only value of this world lay in its power—at certain times—to suggest another world" ("Vastarien," p.20). Those tormented knights of nihilistic faith who, like poor Faliol ("The Masquerade of a Dead Sword," *Heroic Visions II*), have eyes to see beyond this world, may set off in quest of these "zones of fractured numinosity" ("Alice's Last Adventure," p.54), "otherworlds," "little zones," "ultra-mental hinterlands of metaphysics" ("Dream of a Mannikin," p.77). Nathan Jeremy Stein is one such: "a haunter of spectral marketplaces, a visitant of discount houses of unreality, a bargain hunter in the deepest basement of the unknown" ("Notes on the Writing of Horror: A Story," p.160). They are "persons interested in pursuing the existence of utter chaos and mayhem: that is, one of complete liberation at all conceivable levels" ("Ligotti's 'Selections of Lovecraft,'" *Fantasy and Terror #5*, p.22). Like Victor Keirion in "Vastarien" and the narrator of "Les Fleurs," the Ligottian quester sees "keys to an impossible kingdom" (p.29). This is the gnostic quest.

Interestingly, Magister Ligotti warns of two obtacles in the quest of forbidden knowledge. First, one may be too easily satisfied with the cheap trinkets which pose falsely as the bejeweled treasure. Victor Keirion has successfully overpassed this hurdle. He remains firm in "his belief that there existed some other arcana, one of a different kind altogether from that proffered by the books before him, all of which were absorbed in the real, falsely hermetic ventures which consisted of circling the same absurd landscape. The other worlds portrayed in these books inevitably served as annexes or reflections of this one; they were impostors of the authentic unreality which was the only realm of redemption . . ." ("Vastarien," p.21). Similarly, Klaus Klingman must make his pupil first doubt facile claims of the arcane before he can penetrate beyond doubt to the amazing truth.

The other temptation is to tire and become prematurely jaded as the narrator of "The Spectacles in the Drawer" (*Tales of Lovecraftian Horror #2*) does. He reasons that all experiences, marvellous and mundane, finally boil dawn to mere experience so that it is hardly worth striking out from Samsara to reach Nirvana. He dismisses a bit of "Sacred Writ" as a "stupid book" despite the fact that its "mysteries . . . were among the most genuine of their kind," because all such grimoires are judged by him mere will-o'-the-wisps. Each repository of cryptical secrets unlocks deeper levels—of further secrets, which once divined will lead only to a new set of riddles. Each revelation is thus relativised and made anticlimatically mundane in its turn. The chances are slim that the final goal can be attained in the short years of a human life. Thus the bored narrator has given up the gnostic quest and hopes to dissuade his self-appointed disciple Plomb, too. In the same way, the narrator of "The Mystics of Muelenberg" has at length abandoned the quest: "This was in the days when esoteric wisdom seemed to count for something in my mind." (p.32).

Ligotti uses the figure of the mystagogue, the initiator into forbidden knowledge, in almost every short story (and again, we may suspect, we detect a hint of his own role as a horror writer). Some characters obviously play this role: the "crow-man" in "Vastarien," Klaus Klingman In "The Mystics of Muelenberg," the hypnotist in "Drink to Me Only with Labyrinthine Eyes," Dr. Voke, perhaps even Dr. Thoss ("The Troubles of Dr. Thoss"), the wise man Vinge ("The Masquerade of a Dead Sword"), etc. But a moment's thought reveals Alice's father ("We know what that means, don't we?"), the tale-telling, soul-stealing Aunt Elise ("The Christmas Eves of Aunt Elise"), the sectarians of Azathoth and the quartet (in "The Music of the Moon") all seem to be mystagogues as well.

Still closer examination might suggest that in all these cases Ligotti is depicting the mystagogue and her/his disciple as alter egos, with the result that the revelation at story's end is a self-revelation like that of the Muelenbergers who, if only temporarily, let themselves face the truth that some hidden part of their souls already knows. This master disciple identity is made quite explicit in "Dreams of a Mannikin" and "Notes on the Writing of Horror: A Story," where the revealer and the receiver of the revelation are finally shown to be two aspects of the same psyche. The link is implicit in stories in which the disciple repeats the experience of the mystagogue and suddenly finds the mystagogue has disappeared (e.g., "The Music of the Moon," "Dr. Locrian's Asylum," "The Mystics of Muelenberg"). In such cases the disciple replaces the master; the two are one. It is as if, e.g., Klingman is the master in the past and the narrator is the same master at a later point in time. In "The Sect of the Idiot" no sooner does the narrator find the human sectarians' chairs empty than he begins to change physically into one of them.

The most striking example may be "The Spectacles in the Drawer" in which the gullible buffoon Plomb seems to represent the rejected quester-persona of the cynical narrator himself. He scorns his disciple because, unlike himself, the poor "fool" still possesses the zeal to "plumb" the depths from which the narrator has turned away. The mystagogue and the disciple exchange roles, and Plomb finally forces in his former master "mysteries and marvels beyond anything I had ever suspected." Other details confirm this reading as well: at the opening of the story, Plomb ogles the esoteric souvenirs brought back from his master's travels, but by the ending, it is Plomb who has returned from a visionary trip bearing unwelcome gifts of revelation.

Finally, we may briefly consider Ligotti's use of that classic device of horror fiction, the secret or forbidden book. Among the "manuscripts found in lonely places" ("Notes on the Writing of Horror: A Story," p.160) are the *Necronomicon* of Lovecraft, the *Noctuary of Tine* (thusly in "Vastarien," but called "the lost grimoire of the Abbot of Tine" in "The Spectacles in the Drawer") *Cynothoglys*, *Vastarien*, and "the forbidden *Psalms of the Silent.*" The last two are especially interesting because of a modicum of explanation Ligotti supplies.

Of *Vastarien* we are told, intriguingly, that it is "an extremely special book, that is not . . . yes, that is not about something, but actually is that something" (p.22). The volume is even more elusive than Ligotti's own *Songs of a Dead Dreamer:* there is but one single copy that has waited for an untold period for its one destined reader to discover it, a reader who by opening its covers would find it a veritable gateway to the final Nirvana of naught.

Psalms of the Silent is the book without a living author ("The Spectacles in the Drawer"). Wisely, Ligotti never dispels the evocative quality of this title by explaining it, but perhaps we may be permitted a moment or two of exegetical pedantry.

The title might imply that these psalms were learned from the dead, who presumably sing them in silence, learned from them via necromancy, just as Dr. Locrian interrogated the dead. Thus no living author. (In this case, note the equivalence of *Psalms of the Silent* to *Songs of a Dead Dreamer!*)

Or these may be psalms to be chanted silently as Faliol does, recalling how the sectarians of the Idiot seemed to communicate not by their buzzing but by their intermittent silences.

Or perhaps these psalms are "a liturgy of shadows, a catechism of phantoms" ("Vastarien," p. 21) used by a secret sect who are silent, like all true gnostics, toward the outside world because they possess "a knowledge that was unspoken and unspeakable" ("Dr. Locrian's Asylum," p.83).

These tantalizing texts would seem to be only a few of many from Ligotti's library, an archive at least as extensive as the Librairie de Grimoires in "Vastarien" and Locrian's "Strange Library" in "Dr. Locrian's Asylum."

NOTE:

1. All stories collected in *Songs of a Dead Dreamer* are cited from that edition, never in their magazine appearances. Other, uncollected stories are cited by story title and magazine title.

"NOTHING IS WHAT IT SEEMS TO BE": THOMAS LIGOTTI'S ASSAULT ON CERTAINTY

Stefan Dziemianowicz

In his tongue-in-cheek essay "Professor Nobody's Little Lectures on Supernatural Horror," Thomas Ligotti singles out the important role the element of doubt plays in supernatural horror: "Just a little doubt slipped into the mind, a trickle of suspicion in the bloodstream, and all those eyes, one by one, will open to the world, will see its horror as it has never been seen before. Then: no belief or body of laws will guard you; no friend, no counselor, no appointed personage will save you; no crowded schoolroom, no locked bedroom, no bright kitchen will protect you."[1]

Doubt, as readers of supernatural horror fiction know, is essential to the willing suspension of disbelief, the means by which the writer induces the reader to accept the unacceptable. The writer persuades the reader to accept something inconsistent with what the reader knows to be true, usually by creating a fictional world that is consistent with the reader's, save that the supernatural is *not* inconsistent with the characters, situations and events of that world.

In supernatural horror fiction, then, the element of doubt is most often a means to an end, a device the writer uses to neutralize the reader's defenses against unreality just long enough for the specter, the monster, or the supernatural creature to slip through. Where Ligotti departs from most of his contemporaries is in his use of doubt as an end in itself. Rather than depict a world in which the natural and supernatural co-exist side by side, distinct from on another, Ligotti so discomposes the certainty of the "real" world of his stories that characters are forced to redefine what they consider "real" and "unreal," "natural" and "supernatural." Although Ligotti's stories abound with eccentric characters, nightmarish landscapes, even the occasional inhuman creature, it's the overwhelming force of uncertainty running through them that presents the greatest threat: it has as tangible a presence as any supernatural monster, and it sends the vulnerable fleeing from it in terror.

Although Ligotti is best known for his dreamy, metaphysical stories, his most traditional horror tale, "The Frolic," offers a good example of the subtle ways in which he brings the certainty of the familiar world into question. The story opens with a homely domestic scene: Dr. David Munck, a new psychologist at a state penitentiary, is having cocktails with his wife Leslie one evening while their daughter sleeps upstairs. On the surface, all appears to be well-but it isn't. Munck was disturbed that day by a counseling session with a nameless prisoner referred to only as John Doe. Doe has been imprisoned for "frolicking" with children, an act never described but which, from hints of the appearances of bodies found afterward, Munck assumes is a euphemism for an act of criminal perversion.

Doe has told Munck that he wanted to be captured, that he can leave the penitentiary any time he wishes but stays because he finds his incarceration stimulating; also, that "he made the evidence look that way as a deliberate afterthought, that what he really means by 'frolicking' is a type of activity far beyond the crime for which he was convicted." In this familiar madman/sane man stand-off there's no way that Munck can disprove anything that Doe says. Yet there's no doubt in Munck's mind that Doe is a classic psychopath. He bases his diagnosis on the "blasphemous fairyland" in which Doe says he lives and "frolics." Munck tells his wife that Doe

".. . talked about a place that sounded like the back alleys of some cosmic slum, an inner dimensional dead end. Which might be an indication of a ghetto upbringing in Doe's past. And if so, his sanity has transformed these ghetto memories into a realm that cross-breeds a banal streetcorner reality with a psychopath's paradise. This is where he does his 'frolicking' with what he calls his 'awe-struck company', the place probably being an abandoned building of some kind or even an accommodating sewer somewhere. I say this based on his repeated mentioning of a 'jolly river of refuse' and the 'jowled heaps of shadows' which are certainly imaginative transmutations of the local dump. Less fathomable are his memories of a moonlight corridor where mirrors scream and laugh, dark peaks of some kind that won't remain still, a stairway that's 'broken' in a very strange way, though this last one fits in with the background of a dilapidated slum.

"But despite all these dreamy backdrops in Doe's imagination, the mundane evidence of his frolics still points to a crime of very familiar down-to-earth horrors. A run of the mill atrocity.[2]

A trained psychologist, Munck assumes that Doe's world is no more than the product of a "ramshackle ruin of a decaying mind" distorting the images of the normal world. It's impossible for him to concede that because not *everything* Doe describes has a clinical analogue, perhaps Doe isn't raving-that there may actually be something uncanny about him. This in spite of the fact that Doe appears to know something of Munck that he shouldn't: during their dialogue, Doe asked whether Munck had a child of his own, and asked in such a way as to suggest that he knew of Munck's daughter by name. Munck looks in on his own daughter early in the story, sees her sleeping contentedly with her arms wrapped around a stuffed animal, and with that innocent image in his mind comes downstairs to deliver "the wonderfully routine message that Norleen was peacefully asleep." At the end of the story though, when he discovers that the stuffed animal was not purchased by Leslie, Munck returns to his daughter's room, feeling "as if I know something and don't know it at the same time," and finds her gone, the animal disemboweled on the bed, and a note from John Doe attached to it saying that he and Norleen have gone frolicking.

What is it that Munck knows but doesn't know? Quite possibly that he has overestimated the certainty of what he believes to be true. Consciously, Munck has made an effort to fit things he is certain he knows about Doe into what he calls a "pattern of coherency" (i.e., a conventional diagnostic profile), in the hope that, ultimately, the things he is uncertain about will also fall into place. Subconsciously, though, Munck is aware that his own encounter with Doe has left him questioning certainties in his own life.

In response to Leslie's question about how he is after his day at the office, Munck replies:

"Severely, doubting, that's how I am." He said this with a kind of reflectiveness.

"Anything particularly doubtful, Dr. Munck?"

"Only everything," he added.

This casual, seemingly harmless smalltalk between husband and wife takes on ominous meaning as the story progresses, for Munck realizes he has indeed begun to doubt things he once took for granted. As Munck prepares to tell Leslie about his unsettling day, he

> . . . felt his own words lingering atmospherically in the room, tainted with the serenity of the house. Until then, their home had been an insular haven beyond the contamination of the prison, an imposing structure outside the town limits. Now its psychic imposition transcended the limits of physical distance. Inner distance constricted, and David sensed the massive prison walls shadowing the cozy neighborhood outside.[3]

As Munck senses that a refuge he once thought safe is now threatened, the secure borders of the physical world seem to dissolve. In his mind, the real and the imagined have become intermingled.

Woven more deeply into the fabric of the story are ethical and moral ambiguities that come to light in the course of the evening. Leslie, it turns out, has bought a sculpture at the prison workshop to cheer David up. "It was the head of a young boy described in gray formless clay and glossily glazed in blue. The work radiated an extraordinary and intense beauty, the subject's face expressing a kind of ecstatic serenity, the labyrinthine simplicity of a visionary." David recognizes the sculpture, because he "even forced a grudging compliment for the craftsmanship of the thing. It's obviously remarkable." He shocks Leslie when he tells her that the artist is Doe and that the subject of the artwork is "his last-and according to him his most memorable-frolic." Leslie "thought it would help to support those prisoners who are doing something creative instead of . . . destructive things," but David points out to her a dichotomy she never considered: "Creativity isn't always an index of niceness."

Yet David can understand how Leslie, not knowing the background of the sculpture and thus perfectly objective in her appreciation of it, could be attracted to it, for he experienced something of the same clinical detachment, only on a more conscious level, in his converdsation with Doe:

> "The conversation we had could even be called stimulating in a clinical sort of way. He described his 'frolicking' in a kind of unreal and highly imaginative manner that wasn't always hideous to listen to. The strange beauty of this thing in the box here-disturbing as it is-somewhat parallels the language he used when talking about those poor kids. At times I couldn't help being fascinated, though maybe I was shielding my feelings with a psychologist's detachment. Sometimes you have to distance yourself, even if it means becoming a little less human."[4]

Just as there is more than one side to the artwork of John Doe (who, not uncoincidentally, is described as having a multiple personality), so does David reveal a dual personality that's a consequence of his work as a psychologist: it's possible for him to be intrigued professionally by what disgusts him personally.

As these ambiguities accumulate, Ligotti heightens their effect through a playful, almost devious use of puns and double entendres—not the least of which is the real meaning of the term "frolic"—as though to show that even language has a natural inconsistency. It gradually is clear to the reader (if not to David and Leslie) that the reliability and certainty of many commonplace things are qualified by circumstances of the moment: there's no assurance that they won't acquire a different, perhaps completely opposite meaning when viewed at another time, in a different context. In the world as it is presented in "The Frolic," it's difficult to determine anything with *absolute* certainty. Thus, by the end of the story, David—who assured Leslie earlier that "Prisoners like [Doe] don't escape in the normal course of things. They just bounce off the walls but not over them"—admits to uneasiness over the safety of Norleen and the family because "Much of the time I talked to him I had the feeling he was beyond me in some way, I don't know exactly how. I'm sure it was just the customary behavior of the psychopath—trying to shock the doctor. It gives them a sense of power." At this point, though, on the verge of going upstairs to check on Norleen for the last time, David knows he's contradicting himself. He's *not* sure about his family's safety any more than he's sure about anything else he has discussed that evening. At every point where he has sought reinforcement for what he thinks, he has found only contradictions or alternative possibilities. By the story's end he must acknowledge that his self-assurance has blinded him to many uncertainties and that in a world where nothing is absolutely certain, the reality of what John Doe says can be doubted, but it can't be ruled out conclusively.

"The Frolic" ends with the characters realizing they've greatly overestimated the autonomy of what they consider to be real in their own world. In this respect, it's probably the most merciful of Ligotti's tales, which typically end with characters doubting everything they once thought true about their world because they've been swept into some other, incomprehensible but more terrifyingly insistent "reality." It should be noted, though, that in Ligotti's fiction, any given reality is purely an illusion shaped by perception. Characters may eventually come to think of the un-reality in which they become trapped as "more real," and even knowable.

Many of Ligotti's stories evolve out of the relationship perceived between some aspect of the normal world and its opposite. With the slightest inconsistency in the normal world or the least eccentricity on the part of people living in it, the borders between the normal and the abnormal break down, and characters begin to doubt not only the certainty of what they know to be real, but even their own objective existence. The relationship between life and art is at the center of "The Troubles of Dr. Thoss" and "Alice's Last Adventure." The first story tells of Alb Indys, an insomniac artist with no imagination, who appropriates other artists' images and mixes them together in contexts of his own creation. After reading the legend of Dr. Thoss, who was thought to have gone mad but continued to practice medicine (much to the misfortune of his patients), Indys falls asleep. When he wakes up he finds himself in an altered world in which it appears that Dr. Thoss is pursuing him. Indys's grisly death at the end suggests that he himself may have been little more than an image appropriated by someone else and mixed into a scenario concerning the legendary Dr. Thoss. In "Alice's Last Adventure," the woman telling the story is a writer of children's books who was named for the Alice of Lewis Carroll's stories. Recalling the scene where Alice peers into the looking glass and sees a room "not as 'tidy'"as her own, the author likens it to her own untidy life, which has been pocked marked by "nervous breakdown, divorce, remarriage, alcoholism, widowhood, stoic tolerance of a second-rate reality." Her account of several inexplicable experiences in the past years interspersed between the usual disorganized moments of her life leave the reader sensing that her life may just be a less tidy reflection of some more ordered existence being lived elsewhere.

Subjective and objective perceptions of reality are the basis of "The Mystics of Muelenberg" which opens with the narrator offering the following argument:

> If things are not what they seem—and we are forever reminded that this is the case—then it must also be observed that enough of us ignore this truth to keep the world from collapsing. Though never exact, always shifting somewhat, the proportion is crucial.[5]

The narrator, we learn, has been told of a medieval town where, coincidentally, every person's mind "wandered in the shadows" at the same time, so that the unendurable truths underlying their perceptions of reality were revealed. This plants doubt about the real world in the narrator's mind, yet he must remain forever in doubt, for there is no way that he, as an individual, can test the validity of the argument.

All of Ligotti's stories have a psychological focus, especially the paranoia characters feel once they sense that reality is being manipulated by forces beyond them. Since many of his stories are told in the first person, the reader never knows how much to trust the sanity of the narrator. In "Alice's Last Adventure," "The Mystics of Muelenberg," "Dreams of a Mannikin, or a Third Person," and other stories, one might almost say the reader is *encouraged* to suspect the narrator's sanity, helping to establish yet another point of view as to what is happening in the tale. Ligotti explores the point at which boundaries between sanity and insanity become blurred in "Vastarien." This story tells of Victor Keirion, who seeks access to the world of dreams through a book a mysterious man buys for him. Keirion kills the man when he discovers the book was bought only so that the man could steal from Keirion the dreams that he (the man) himself can't have. At the end of the story, whose events have unfolded through Keirion's eyes, it is revealed that Keirion is imprisoned in an insane asylum for having committed the murder. Was the man, as Keirion claims, "using him in a horrible way, a way impossible to explain or to make credible?" Or is Keirion just a madman who killed someone and then fabricated an elaborate rationale for doing so? Either possibility is arguable.

The opposite reality of which Ligotti seems to be fondest is the world of dreams. The relationship between reality and dream in his stories is summed up in a passage from "Vastarien," in which Victor Keirion compares the town he sees in waking life to the dreamworld of the title:

> Victor Keirion belonged among those possessed of the conviction that the only value of this world lay in its power—at certain times—to suggest another world. Nevertheless, the place he now surveyed through the high window could never be anything but the most gauzy phantom of the other place, nothing save a shadowy mimic of the anatomy of that great dream. And although there were indeed times when one might be deceived, isolated moments when a gift for disguise triumphs, the impersonation could never be perfect or lasting. No true challenge to the rich unreality of Vastarien, where every shape suggested a thousand others and every sound disseminated everlasting echoes, every word founded a world. No horror, no joy was the equal of the abysmally vibrant sensations known in this place that was elsewhere, a place where all experiences were interwoven to compose fantastic textures of feeling, a fine and dark tracery of limitless patterns. For everything in the unreal points to the infinite, and everything in Vastarien was unreal, unbounded by the tangible lie of existing.[6]

In Ligotti's dream stories, it's the very surreality of dreams-their capacity to make the smallest detail seem representative of something larger than life, something that transcends mundane existence-that makes them seem more real than waking life. However, it must be said that characters who encounter the dream world are grossly unequipped to deal with this immensity, and find that their experiences leave them bereft of any sense of a familiar, ordered reality. "The Sect of the Idiot" opens with its narrator arriving in his idealized conception of a small town, which he refers to, ironically, as "a land of dreams." He derives "a sense of serene enclosure" from the town's overhanging roofs and balconies. "Even the infinite nights above the great roofs of the town seemed merely the uppermost level of an earthbound estate, at most a musty old attic in which the stars were useless heirlooms and the moon a dusty trunk of a dream." At the same time that it's a "claustrophobe's nightmare," "the town also conveyed a sense of endlessness." For the narrator, "this paradox was precisely the source of the town's enchantment."

That evening, the narrator has an unusual dream that opens him up to a sense of the vastness beyond his idealized perception:

> I felt that unseen things were taking place in obscure corners of this scene, none of them having any kind of reality to them, all of them vague and carried out in a state of sluggish inertia . . . I seemed to be an unseen speck lost in a convoluted festival of strange schemes. And it was this very remoteness from the designs of my dream universe, this feeling of fantastic homelessness amid a vast alien pattern, that was the source of unnameable and possibly limitless terrors.[7]

Indeed, the narrator feels so alienated within his dream that he's almost displaced out of it: "nothing supported my existence, which I felt at any moment might be horribly altered or simply . . . ended. In the profoundest meaning of the expression, my life was of no matter."

In this dream, the narrator is drawn to a room that he senses is submerged in a different time stream, yet is "no different from any of the old rooms, the high and lonely rooms I had known in waking life, even if *this* room seemed to border on the voids of space and time and its windows opened onto the infinite outside." Inside this room the narrator is appalled to find a group of hooded, tentacled creatures who inspire in him a vision:

> This revelation—in keeping with the style of certain dreams—was complicated and exact, allowing no ambiguities or confusions to comfort the dreamer. And what was imparted to my witnessing mind was the vision of a world in a trance; a hypnotized parade of being sleepwalking to the odious manipulations of their whispering masters, those hooded freaks *who were themselves among the hypnotized*. For there was a power superseding theirs, a power which they served and from which they emanated, something which was beyond the universal hypnosis by virtue of its very mindlessness, its awesome idiocy. These cloaked masters, in turn, partook in some measure of godhead, passively presiding as enlightened zombies over the multitudes of the entranced, that frenetic domain of the human sphere.[8]

Upon awakening, the narrator finds himself looking at the world from an entirely new perspective. "The streets that I looked upon that motionless morning were filled with new secrets and seemed to lead into the very essence of the extraordinary . . . And somehow this undercurrent of deception, of corruption in disguise, served to intensify the town's most attractive aspects." But then he comes upon the room he saw in his dreams, and find that it looks unnervingly the same. There are no hooded figures, but there is a little man whom he encountered at another place the day before. The man now appears "to be no more than a malignant puppet of madness," and he tells the narrator that he belongs to the hooded ones, and that the transformation is slowly taking over his entire body.

As is usual with Ligotti's fiction, the interpretation of this story is left open. The narrator's conclusion that "I have been lured away by dreams; all is nonsense now" suggests that he believes his dreams have lead him into madness. Yet, his lament that "to suffer a solitary madness seems the joy of paradise when compared to the extraordinary condition in which one's own madness is merely an echo from the world outside" implies that he senses an even more profound dilemma: if he is not really mad, if his perceptions are actually an echo from the outside world, then that world is utterly intolerable. For what the narrator has come to understand is that the world and the people in it, including himself, may be no more than characters in the dreams of the hooded ones (who themselves may be figments of something else's dream). This realization is supported amply, though not conclusively, by what he felt during his dream: his personal sense of insignificance and the familiarity of the room of the hooded ones. It's as though in his dream, he was awakened to a reality to which he was oblivious, but in which he has been participating all his life. This could account for the different appearance of the town upon his awakening and especially for his perception of another human being, who is not similarly enlightened, as "a puppet of madness". The end of the story leaves him trapped in the self-awareness that, at the same time he exists apart from this world, he is a part of it.

The sudden self-consciousness of characters that they are only passive figures not in control of their world is crystallized in the image of the puppet or manikin, a recurrent motif in stories like "The Sect of the Idiot," "Dr. Voke and Mr. Veech" and especially in "Dreams of a Mannikin, or the Third Person," possibly Ligotti's most chilling deconstruction of reality. In this story, a psychoanalyst writes to a professional colleague with occult interests about Amy Locher, a patient the colleague referred to him. Amy, who says she is a secretary in waking life, tells the analyst of a dream she had in which her job consisted of dressing manikins in a store window. As the mannikin dresser, she has a dream in which she finds herself in a hallway that is supposed to be her bedroom, but is full of "people dressed as dolls . . . some of them have actually become dolls . . . others are at various intermediate stages between humanness and dollhood." To her horror, she realizes that she is posed in exactly the same posture as the dolls. When a menacing presence grabs her from behind and speaks to her in the same type of voice *she* uses when dressing mannikins in her "waking" life, she awakens directly back into her life as Amy Locher-but upon looking behind her she sees a mannikin torso, jutting through the headboard, that only gradually withdraws back into the wall.

The psychoanalyst theorizes that Amy's nightmare is redolent of the solipsistic dream of Chuang Tzu—who awoke one morning from dreaming that he was a butterfly, and could not be sure that he wasn't a butterfly dreaming he was a man—only to dismiss it. One would know when one was dreaming, says the doctor, since "the horrific feeling of unreality is much more prevalent (to certain people) in what we call human 'reality' than in human dreams, where everything is absolutely real"—what Ligotti describes in "Vastarien" as "nightmare made normal." The psychoanalyst offers another explanation for the dreams of Chuang Tzu, which it turns out is also a pet theory of the occultist friend: "that which you call 'divine masochism,' or the doctrine of a Bigger Self terrorizing its little splinter selves, precisely that Something Else Altogether scarifying the man-butterfly with uncanny suspicions that there's a game going on over its collective head."

The psychoanalyst has reason to suspect that his occultist friend either planted this notion in Amy Locher through post-hypnotic suggestion, or that Amy and the friend are conspiring to upset him. For when Amy failed to come to her second appointment and he went to search out the address she gave him, he found it to be for a clothing store, with a mannikin in the window that looks exactly like her. When the he confirms from a nearby phone booth that the phone number Amy gave him is indeed the number to that store (one at which he discovers his friend buys clothes), he notes how "It seemed you might have accomplices anywhere, and to tell you the truth I was beginning to feel a bit paranoid standing in that phone booth." Driving home he thinks he sees something in his backseat, but upon turning around he finds nothing. "But the point is I had to check in order to relieve my moment of anxiety," he admits. "You had succeeded, my love, in getting me to experience a moment of self-terror, and in that moment I too became your accomplice against myself." The psychoanalyst also began having dreams like Amy Locher's, in which he finds himself in an attic room full of "people dressed as dolls," who invite him to "'Become as we are . . . Die into us.'"

The story ends with the psychoanalyst observing:

> Consciously, of course, I still uphold the criticism I've already expressed about the basic silliness of your work. Uncon-

sciously, however, you seem to have awakened me to a stratum (*zone,* you would say) of uncanny terror in my mind-soul. I will at least admit that your ideas form a powerful psychic metaphor, though no more than that . . . Suppose that I admit that she somehow was just a dream . . . Suppose I even admit that Miss Locher was not a girl, but actually a multi-selved *thing*—part Man, part Mannikin—and with your assistance, reproduced itself for a time into existence, reproduced itself in human form just as we reproduce ourselves with an infnite variety of images and shapes, including mannikins. You would like to have me think things like this. You would like to have me think of all the mysterious connections between different things.[9]

The one suspicion the psychoanalyst doesn't voice—the one with which the story ends—is the one he is obviously laboring to rationalize away: that he is a smaller self who has suddenly become aware he is being terrorized by a larger self "splintering and scaring itself to relieve its cosmic ennui"—in other words, that he and his entire world are merely a fictional diversion created by some incomprehensible Other.

Ligotti has written one tale which is not told from the victim's point of view. It would be unique for this reason alone, but in it Ligotti also explores what might be termed the ultimate breakdown between reality and unreality. "Drink to Me Only with Labyrinthine Eyes" is the account of a mesmerist hired to provide entertainment for "fancy persons at a fancy house." The mesmerist is not fooled by all of his audience's pomp and decoration: he observes that, "despite all the wealth, prestige and honors mingling in this rather baroque room tonight, I think they know how basically ordinary they all are." The mesmerist comes to this conclusion after the show he has just presented. He has put his assistant Seraphita, a somnambule, through the usual paces, having her perform contortions that seem possible only under the power of hypnosis. As a finale, he attempts to transform his assistant before the audience's eyes, into an angelic image of "celestiality discarnate." The image lasts but a moment and when the audience responds with only perfunctory applause, the mesmerist reasons, "They don't understand. They actually like all the mock-death and bogus-pain stuff better. These are what fascinates them."

This echoes an observation Ligotti makes in his incarnation as Professor Nobody, that we all have a natural fascination with horror as a consequence of being "both victims and witnesses to this gruesome circus of living tissue." As the only creatures on earth who are self-conscious of their own morbidity and mortality, humans have an ambivalent relationship with supernatural horror. In one sense, part of us finds in it "a simple and necessary justification of the inevitable." Yet another part of us wants to "keep us from being absolute victims, striving to avoid our doom." It's in our failure to admit that "a sense of beauty and order, compassion for human hurt, offering others the benefit rather than the disadvantage of our doubts, nurturing a rich respect for the phenomena of decency and nobility—all of our best attributes are also our most troublesome and serve to bolster, not assuage horror" that we indulge "a penchant for self-torment, or mania to preserve a demented innocence in the face of gruesome facts."

This is what the mesmerist finds so "ordinary" about his audience: their fascination with "the mock death and bogus-pain stuff" only reveals them to be obsessed with the underlying reality of their own mortality, no matter how much their extravagant lifestyles seem to deny it. So he intends to fulfill their unspoken wish. Seraphita, it turns out, is not the hypnotic subject—rather, she's a corpse whom the mesmerist has everyone believing is beautiful. Musing on mortality, the mesmerist notes how, "It is said that death is great awakening, an emergence from the trance of life. Ha, I have to laugh. Death is the consummation of mortality and—to let out a big secret—only heightens mortal susceptibilities." Seen in this light, Seraphita is not the opposite of the living partygoers, but a more intensified expression of them. By the illusion of her beauty that he sustains, the mesmerist is all but saying that life itself is nothing more than a dream momentarily obscuring the reality of death.

The scene with which the story end is unsettling to say the least: as he has done at many other parties before, the mesmerist has left a posthypnotic suggestion for the partygoers that they will awaken at the sound of a chime. With Seraphita inside, the mesmerist stands outside on the front porch, his fingers poised over the doorbell. "We showed them what you could be, O Serpahita," he muses, "now let's show them what you really are." There is perhaps no better image than this to sum up Thomas Ligotti's approach to supernatural horror. For one can see in the mesmerist's desire to cater to his audience's tastes-morbid as they may be—a resemblance to Ligotti the storyteller. And one can't miss the suggestion here, as in the rest of his fiction, that he considers what we call reality to be little more than a dream from which we, his readers, are about to be rudely awakened.

NOTES:

1. Thomas Ligotti, *Songs of a Dead Dreamer*. (Albuquerque, NM: Silver Scarab Press, 1985), p. 142.
2. Ibid, pp. 17-18.
3. Ibid, p. 11.
4. Ibid, pp. 16-17.
5. *Crypt of Cthulhu* #51, Hallowmas 1987, p. 32.
6. *Crypt of Cthulhu* #48, St. John's Eve 1987, pp. 20-21.
7. *Crypt of Cthulhu* #56, Roodmas 1988, p. 12.
8. Ibid, p. 14
9. *Songs of a Dead Dreamer.*

DISILLUSIONMENT CAN BE GLAMOROUS: AN INTERVIEW WITH THOMAS LIGOTTI

E.M. Angerhuber and Thomas Wagner

TW/EMA: Mr. Ligotti, how are you?

Ligotti: A simple question, but for some reason it triggers something I once read in Kafka's letters. Kafka remarked to a correspondent that his emotional state was so unstable that, as he stood at the bottom of a flight of stairs, he had no idea how he would feel when he had reached to the top of the stairs. Anyway, in answer to your question, I'm not feeling too bad at the moment.

TW: If you may have heard this questions several times before: what was your motive to begin writing? What was it that evoked your fascination for the horror genre—what caused you to write such stories?

Ligotti: Since I was a child I've had a morbid and melodramatic imagination. I went to see every horror movie at the local theaters and stayed up late to watch midnight horror movies on TV. As a teenager I had a tendency to depression. To me, the world was just something to escape from. I started escaping with alcohol and then, as the sixties wore on, with every kind of drug I could get. In August of 1970 I suffered the first attack of what would become a lifelong anxiety-panic disorder. Not too long after that I discovered the works of H. P. Lovecraft. I found that the meaningless and menacing universe described in Lovecraft's stories corresponded very closely to the place I was living at that time, and ever since for that matter. I was grateful that someone else had perceived the world in a way similar to my own view. A few years later, when I took an interest in writing fiction, there was never a question that I would write anything else other than horror stories.

TW: You are an open admirer of H.P. Lovecraft and Bruno Schulz' works. While I can only recognize a faint Lovecraft influence on your stories—mainly the image of a black, omnipotent universe and the impotence of the characters—Schulz may occupy a wider space in your work. In general, I could say that there is a "kafkaesque" (or simply odd) atmosphere in your stories that I chiefly know from European authors like Franz Kafka, Jean Ray, Leo Perutz, Arthur Machen . . . Have you been inspired by them? Or does this odd atmosphere simply result from your own point of view?

Ligotti: From around 1975 I became very interested in the figures and trends of foreign literatures, especially nineteenth- and twentieth-century French literature from the Decadent-Symbolism movement through Surrealism. These movements and the writers associated with them influenced every other literature in the world, with the exception of American literature. Sadeq Hedayat in Iran, Hagiwara Sakutaro in Japan, Spanish-American writers like Ruben Dario, just about every Russian author from the 1890s until the 1917 revolution, and on and on. They all looked to such French writers as Baudelaire, Verlaine, and Huysmans as literary models. And so did I.

EMA: You've also mentioned two other important literary models, Thomas Bernhard and Vladimir Nabokov. In which way did they affect your work?

Ligotti: The work of both of these authors frequently features mentally deranged narrators who write highly stylized prose. In this sense they are part of a tradition that also includes Poe and Lovecraft. Those are the footsteps in which I often slavishly followed.

EMA: What was the title of the first story you published? Do you harbour any special emotions for this particular story?

Ligotti: The first story of mine to be published was "The Chymist," which appeared in Harry Morris's legendary fanzine *Nyctalops* in 1980. I don't really harbor any special emotions for any of my stories.

EMA: How did the recognition you earned for your literary work affect the circumstances of your life or the way you see yourself? What does it feel like to be a "cult author"?

Ligotti: I was very relieved when my stories were well-received by readers of small press magazines and, later, by critics who reviewed my collections. I wanted to be a writer in the fashion of Lovecraft, and until I attained some recognition for my horror stories I could barely stand to live with myself. It was something that I really needed to get out of my system. So, as I said, I was very relieved within myself when I achieved my modest literary ambitions. But as far as the circumstances of my life are concerned, nothing really changed. I go to work every day like most people. I wonder what's going to become of me if I live into old age since one doesn't become rich or famous just by writing short horror stories. As for being a cult author, I've said this many times to people: "There's no obscurity like minor renown." Not that I mind obscurity in the least. I wouldn't want to be well known to a wide public. I'd rather acquire millions of dollars playing the lottery than by writing best-selling books. Don't misunderstand me—as I mentioned before, I wanted to be published in the worst way and I craved attention for what I had written. That is true for just about anyone who writes. Poor Poe openly declared that he lusted for a level of fame that he never saw in his lifetime. But I've already gotten all the fame I can handle at the moment, thanks.

EMA: Do you have any favourite stories among your own *oeuvre*? If yes, what is it you like most in them?

Ligotti: I usually name "The Shadow at the Bottom of the World" when I'm asked this question. In that story I think I wrote something subtle and mysterious while still managing to stay within the horror genre, which I've always been concerned to do.

TW: The first Ligotti story I ever read was "Drink To Me Only With Labyrinthine Eyes," and it seemed to me like a blend of Poe and Kafka. It's a strange story that still touches me with its bizarre beauty. Just recently I've discovered that there is an old song entitled "Drink To Me Only With Thine Eyes." Thus, one may suspect that the title of your story hasn't been chosen by mere coincidence. If you know the song I'm referring to, is this only a play on words, or is there more to tell?

Ligotti: At the time I wrote that story I was reading a lot of English and European poets of the seventeenth century. These poets, including Gongora in Spain and Metaphysical Poets like Donne and Marvell in England, were renowned for writing in a somewhat flamboyant style and approaching traditional poetic forms in new and often strange ways. The poetry of Ben Jonson and some of the English Cavelier Poets also displays these qualities to some extent. It was from the lyric by Jonson that borrowed, in a mutated form, the title "Drink to Me Only with Labyrinthine Eyes."

EMA: One of your books has the title *Noctuary*. I've always been wondering if this word is derived from "sanctuary" or rather from "diary" . . .

Ligotti: It's derived from diary. I thought I had invented the word until I found it in the *Oxford English Dictionary*.

EMA: My favourite vignette from *Noctuary* is "The Eternal Mirage," a very abstract, very unreal and exceptionally beautiful piece. What was your motive to write it this way?

Ligotti: With that piece I wanted to convey my sense of the universe as something thin and unstable, something that barely has the quivering and illusory quality of a mirage and yet, alas, refuses to dissolve completely into nothingness.

EMA: Your story "The Bungalow House" is partially based on real events—could you please tell us something about the mysterious Bungalow Bill and his tapes?

Ligotti: The first of the "Bungalow House" tapes is based on an actual dream I had which I tried to describe as accurately as possible when I woke up, something I had never done before and haven't done since. Later I developed the transcript of that dream into a story and invented some more dreams to go along with it. The idea of a so-called performance artist reading these "dream monologues" into a tape recorder was inspired by actual cassette tapes that I and my coworkers used to find left on a bench near the building where we worked in downtown Detroit.

They were tapes of an elderly man reading from various sources, including the local newspaper, the works of Sigmund Freud, and librettos from Gilbert and Sullivan operettas. These readings were often interrupted by mad laughter. Later some of us, including me, saw and heard the guy who was leaving these tapes, which were always placed inside envelopes taken from a local bank. These were the sort of envelopes bank's offer to customers who want something in which to put their cash withdrawals. On the outside of the envelopes this eldery gentleman, who walked around mumbling and laughing to himself, would write strange phrases, which unfortunately I can't recall any longer, as well as the source material from which the reading on the tape was taken. Bungalow Bill, a name given to him by David Tibet, would leave these envelopes on benches along the sidewalks in downtown Detroit, securing the envelopes in place with then weight of several pennies. He was a rather distinguished, professorial looking guy . . . and he was most certainly insane.

EMA: Did you ever talk to Bill, or otherwise get direct inspiration for your story by him? And what has become of the tapes?

Ligotti: Since the company I work for moved out of Detroit several years ago, those of us who were following Bungalow Bill's tape-recorded monologues lost track of him. None of us ever talked to him or bothered him in any way. I once heard him mumbling and laughing while I was waiting for an elevator. I recognized his voice immediately as he approached me. It couldn't have been anyone else.

EMA: In a short story by Daniel Charms, there is a character named Faol. Could there be any possible link to the character Faliol in your tale "Masquerade of a Dead Sword"?

Ligotti: The name Faliol is a permutation on the name of a character in a play by the Belgian dramatist Michel de Ghelderode.

TW: Many of your narratives are dominated by style, and atmosphere, rather than by plot. . . . In Germany, this "lack of plot" is a popular target for some critics. What is your intention? *L'art pour l'art?* Are your tales reflections of your own emotions, pictures written down straight from out of your head? Do you follow a certain principle, or a certain way of action when writing stories?

Ligotti: I don't understand why people can't see that plot is as fundamental to my stories, with the possible exception of some of my short prose pieces, as it is those of any other horror writer. I don't start writing a story until I know all the principal plot points and their resolution at the end of the tale. What I don't do is structure my stories in such a way that my plots development almost exclusively through dialogue, which is the common practice. The reason for this is that most of my stories are told in the first person by a narrator whose consciousness I always want out front where the reader can see and feel it. Most readers don't like this type of story. They don't want to be reminded that they're reading a story at all, which is why very few best-selling novels are written in the first person.

EMA: In some of your earlier stories, the main character possesses a kind of dark power; later on, the Lovecraftian image of a cosmic evil becomes predominant. Do you think that cosmic evil is an enhanced or higher form of horror, compared to the evil of a single character?

Ligotti: I think that both sources of evil and horror are present in my stories, although in a given story one may seem more prominant than the other. For example, in my early story "The Chymist," the title character is one of those you refer to as possessing a "dark power." But that power is only a instance of a greater power always at large. Simon Smirk, the chemist, openly refers to the power of the Great Chemists of the universe that he is only emulating. The specific power he's referring to is Nature, which tirelessly produces mutations and permutations using human flesh, which is exactlty what Simon himself does in the story. But I think I know what you mean. My earlier main characters do seem to be a far more hellraising bunch than my later main characters, who may be a bit sinister, like the narrator of "Teatro Grottesco," but also end of suffering at the hands of forces more powerful and sinister than they can ever hope to be.

TW: You've been working for quite a couple of years for a big

American publishing house. Did you ever dream of being a professional writer, or do you think you could live with the restrictions a professional writer has to surrender to? I think, as soon as art changes into a job, there's an end to individual freedom.

Ligotti: I realized a long time ago that I could never be a professional writer for the simple reason that I'm not interested in the same things that people who buy the majority of the books in this world are interested in. Like Lovecraft, I'm not interested in people and their relationships. That alone counts me out as a professional writer. I also have a bad attitude toward the world. I think that life is a curse and so on. People reading a book on a beach or in an airplane don't want to hear stuff like that. They just want to relax and be told a diverting story from a third-person omniscient viewpoint, giving them the sense that they have a movie playing in their mind. I don't blame them in the least.

EMA: Your job demands a high amount of responsibility from you. Do you feel comfortable with having responsibility?

Ligotti: I have a low-tolerance for pressure of any kind.

TW: Did you ever have the feeling that writing turns into a torture? Speaking for myself, I know that it gets quite difficult to banish everyday's junk and try to write down a couple of sensible words . . .

Ligotti: To me the actual task of writing is a real pain in the ass. I've fantasized about just imagining the characters and incidents of a story and having it appear in written form before my eyes. I know that there are plenty of writers who genuinely enjoy the nuts and bolts of the literary process. I'm not one of them. I really don't even think of myself as a writer. Probably the only people who think our themselves as writers are the pros who are doing it everyday and have "writer" on their tax forms and passports as their occupation. They're constantly being reminded by one thing or another that they're writers.

TW: Some years ago, Poppy Z. Brite wrote a nice introduction to *The Nightmare Factory* which starts with the words "Are you out there, Thomas Ligotti?" You are surrounded by the image of a anthropophobic hermit; some people even write about you like you were one of your own story characters—at least this is the case in Germany. . . . What does it feel like to be called the "Prince of Dark Fantasy?"

Ligotti: Unless I'm in a state of depression, anxiety, or panic, it feels pretty good when someone speaks well of my work in print. But the effect wears off very fast. Nonetheless, I'm certainly not immune to the powers of either praise or criticism. I wish I were. On the other hand, I don't go around thinking, "Here I am, the Prince of Dark Fantasy—make way for me." You need a lot of sycophants and a lot of money to think like that.

TW: Your stories are quite uncompromising. Either the reader feels cast under their spell and loses himself in the Ligottian cosmos, or he doesn't care for them at all. I think that your aficionados must feel a very special affinity to your work; it's not just entertainment for them. Many readers seem to recognise themselves in your stories, their doubts and fears. Do you think that your stories have influence on their way of thinking? That they might possibly regard them as a kind of philosophy?

Ligotti: I really don't have much contact with people who read my stories. Judging from those with whom I have carried on a more or less regular correspondence, I find that they were attracted to my stories in the first place because they recognized in them something of their own way of thinking. That's how it was when I first read Lovecraft. That's how it works. There's obviously a literary expression of Lovecraft's attitudes and ideas in his writing, as there is in mine. It's probably impossible to write anything without betraying something that someone would call a philosophy. The philosophy of most writers happens to be this: In the world there is good and there is evil, but overall there's more good than evil. That's not how I see things at all. Mine is a minority view, which, for better orn worse, is what I believe you mean by the words "Ligottian cosmos." It's also what distinguishes my writing from that of most authors. In fact it distinguishes my way of thinking from that of most people, including almost all of those people who read and enjoy my stories.

EMA: Are there many fans who try to get in contact with you? What does it mean to you to touch the hearts of people you don't know?

Ligotti: You might imagine, it can be very moving.

EMA: Have you ever felt so deeply touched by another artist's work that you wrote him/her an admiring letter?

Ligotti: Only once. When I was in my early twenties, I wrote a couple fan letters to Joseph Payne Brennan expressing my admiration for what I called his "unabashedly pessimistic" poetry. At the same time I told him that I felt his stories fell far short of his poems. He wrote back to me both times, very patiently and graciously explaining that writing fiction and writing poetry were two different things to him-that his stories were written for largely commercial gain, whereas his poetry was a more genuine expression of himself. I still have the letters.

TW: Up to now, there haven't been many publications of your work in Germany. What about other foreign publications? We've discovered an ad for a Greek publication of *The Nightmare Factory* on a Greek website.

Ligotti: The collections translated into German and Greek are the only foreign-language appearances of my stories, if you don't count translated anthologies in which a story of mine appeared. There was interest at one time in Italian and French translations of my collections, but my publisher either didn't respond to these inquiries or they refused to grant permission for translations of my of my stuff because there really isn't much money to be made from them.

TW: We live in a time of all-embracing fast food. In my opinion, mankind is certainly not more stupid than in former eras, but today there's more food for existing dumbness, and the media and many artists sell themselves in an increasingly extreme way, in every respect. Shit sells best, no matter if you produce literature, music or movies. What is it that goes to make up good literature for you? Or, in your view, what goes to make up art? Are there any living artists whom you admire?

Ligotti: The last great literary hero of mine was William S. Burroughs, and he's been dead for some time now. I'm really very cynical about art with a capital "A" versus popular art. If you stand a certain distance away, which is the only place to stand, it all looks much the same. I patronize popular art in the form of movies and television. I have favorite movies and TV shows. But no movie or TV show will ever be able to provide me with the near fathomless pleasures I've derived, for example, from the stories of Jorge Luis Borges and Dino Buzzati, the essays of E. M. Cioran, or the poetry of Giacomo Leopardi. However, in the end, it's all just entertainment.

TW: When I heard of your collaborations with David Tibet/Current 93, this was quite a discovery for me—two uncompromising exceptional artists meeting. David Tibet's experimental music may seem as "demanding" to many people as your stories. . . . I think both your work harmonizes very well; I've detected a similar atmosphere in both your stories and Tibet's music. How did you come to those collaborations?

Ligotti: One day I received a package containing most of Current 93's discography and a letter from David Tibet expressing admiration for my stories. He also asked if I'd like to collaborate with him on a project. I listened to the CD's, recognized that there were significant similarities between Current 93's songs and my stories, and said I'd be glad to collaborate in some way with him.

EMA: Do you have plans for futher collaborations for the foreseeable future? With David Tibet or with other artists? Do you like to collaborate with somebody else and if yes, why?

Ligotti: I wrote a connected series of pieces with the title "This Degenerate Little Town." At some time in the future, when other projects and committments allow, this will form a third collaboration between myself and David Tibet.

TW: *In a Foreign Town* . . . is a very special book for me. It seems almost like a reappraisal, or a kind of quintessence of many former stories. After having read this book, I had the feeling that something had come full circle. And somehow it seemed to me as if you had reached a climax in your black microcosmos of human puppets, a climax that marked an end, perhaps even a turning point in your work. After you keep intensifying the reader's fascination for the strange "town near the northern border" throughout all of the stories, you finally reveal it as a "genius of the most insidious illusions." The main character decides to "just walk away in silence," and he writes: "I was tired and felt the ache of every broken dream I had ever carried within me." This sounds very disillusioning—the dark, glamourous nightmare crumbles into dust, it's almost like the prosaic sobering up after an LSD trip . . .

Ligotti: I had experienced that sort of disillusionment years earlier. The story "The Spectacles in the Drawer" long preceeds *In a Foreign Town* in conveying this disaffection. But disillusionment can be glamorous too. Anything can be. I would go so far as to say that something absolutely negative, something that has no affirmation whatever at its base, is an impossibility. Even murder and suicide are very positive, very vital and affirmative. There really is no way to escape being pulled into the machine of human existence. Or none that I can conceive of at this time.

TW: Jesters, and harlequins usually appear in your stories as weird, threatening beings, yet your protagonists often seem to be fascinated by them. . . . In the narrative "The Last Feast of Harlequin" the main character loves to dress up as a clown, which finally doesn't do him much good. In "The Bells Will Sound Forever" you display this element in a masterly fashion: the main character, Mr. Crumm, discovers a clown costume in the attic of the mysterious Mrs. Pyk's house. He puts the costume on and finds himself to be a "head on a stick held in the wooden hand of Mrs. Pyk." Crumm—who is actually engaged in the prosaic profession of a commercial agent—seems to feel a bizarre pleasure when putting on someone else's hide, especially that of a jester. But eventually he ends up as an abused puppet-like object. What about yourself? Do you feel intrigued by masks, by the idea of putting on someone else's hide?

Ligotti: My own fantasies of stepping into the skin of another person are much more banal. When I was a kid I wanted to be a baseball player named Rocky Calavito and imitated his batting stance and swing, pretending that I was him. Later I wanted to be any number of rock music stars. And then I wanted to be H. P. Lovecraft. At this time I've run out of other people that I want to be. My ideal persona these days is that of an inmate in a minimum security prison. That really seems like the good life to me.

TW: Another element that keeps re-appearing in your work is the puppet—the conception of being surrounded by puppet-like, doll-like humans, respectively finding oneself transformed into such a being—so to say, bereft of the jester's mask . . . The puppets in your stories seem to me like symbols of the main character's hopelessness. Any attempt to change our destiny is futile because we all are marionettes of a superior dark power. Is Thomas Ligotti a fatalist?

Ligotti: Oh, yeah. Absolutely. . .in principle. In fact, I'm just another sucker like everyone else. I get carried away all the time and desire things that only drag me deeper into the trap of human existence. I'm very attached to members of my family, for instance. And obviously I still write horror stories every once in a while. That's not going to help me when I really need it. There really isn't any difference between me and some religious fundamentalist who thinks about attaining ill-defined state of salvation and then existing forever in a blissful afterlife. Even to carry on until tomorrow is act of ecstatic lunacy, since every tomorrow just brings you closer to that last one, which will probably not shape up to be a very good day.

TW: I've heard that it was your primary dream to become a rock star. Is music still important in your life, does it perhaps even inspire your stories?

Ligotti: The only important thing in my life is to avoid suffering any more pain than I have to and to assist people who are close to me in doing the same. . .in principle. In fact, music has been a significant diversion for me from the time a got my first transitor radio and heard those dopey songs from the early sixties which now sound so haunting to me. "Popsicles and Icicles" is a tune that particularly stands out, as beautiful and otherworldly as something by the Cocteau Twins. I don't think that music has had any direct influence on my stories, except perhaps in some cryptic way that even I don't recognize. I have on occasion tried to conceive of a work of fiction that would have the intensity and impact of a musical composition. But writing doesn't work that way. Its effect on people is weaker but more intimate than that of music. Music seems to come from a million miles away, while writing is inside you.

TW: On the other hand, I find it quite interesting how many musicians seem to be inspired by your writing. I've launched two virtual radio stations at www.MP3.com to feature experimental music which could serve as fictitious scores to your tales. I was amazed of the great amount of interest I received. Many MP3 artists are very fond of your work; others didn't know you but felt appealed by the quoted text pieces and sent me music which harmonized perfectly with your writing. While most horror best sellers seem to be read by housewives, Thomas Ligotti appears to attract to a quite different audience.

Ligotti: I wonder if all of that is really true. I would bet that popular horror writers have their fans among musicians. Heck, Stephen King actually played on the same stage with Al Kooper, one of my idols from the sixties for his work with the Blues Project and Blood, Sweat and Tears. I can even testify to one outstanding instance of a serious musician who reads popular horror. I once read an interview with the jazz bass player Ron Carter, who played with Miles Davis and is definitely no housewife, and in that interview he spoke of his interest in and admiration for the horror novels of Robert McCammon. Who knows-Carter might have composed some complex jazz piece inspired by the work of McCammon. Of course that doesn't detract one bit from those musicians who have honored me with their attention and talents-it just puts it into perspective.

TW: In *The Agonizing Resurrection of Victor Frankenstein & Other Gothic Tales*, your inspirations are taken—among others—from classic horror films. I had the feeling that you know those films very well, perhaps even love them?

Ligotti: You're right. I did know and love them very much when I was young.

EMA: The ruin in "Dr. Locrian's Asylum" does resemble, in a certain way, the settings of old Frankenstein movies: the large table with straps; the creation of something that's "without fate or spirit," and that manages to escape and threaten the townspeople. The Frankenstein Monster is, in a way, the prototype of literary automatons or androids, which could be regarded as the primary model for the (sentient?) puppets that people so much of your stories.

Ligotti: I never thought about the Frankenstein monster that way, but your analysis seems very solid to me.

TW: Do you still find inspiration in films nowadays? When reading your stories, I often see movie-like pictures inside my head—mostly something between *Eraserhead* and *Dr. Caligari* . . .

Ligotti: I loved *The Cabinet of Dr. Caligari* when I saw still photos from the movie in *Famous Monsters* magazine. When I finally saw the movie I thought, "What a bunch of junk and nonsense this is." But I still retained my imaginary, ideal version of *Caligari* and have injected that version into some of my tales. I'm not aware of any direct influence of newer horror movies on my stories. I can't think of the last good horror movie I saw. Probably *Alien* or John Carpenter's *The Thing*, whichever was more recent.

TW: Speaking of the subject, you've written two film scripts in collaboration with Brandon Trenz which have unfortunately not been filmed yet, "Crampton" (an *X-Files* episode) and "The Last Feast of Harlequin" (which is based on your story of the same name). What made you do that, apart from the financial aspect? Which emotions does the idea of getting one of your stories filmed imply?

Ligotti: Writing "Crampton," which has been rewritten as a non-*X-Files* feature film, was something that I thought would be fun, which it was because it was a successful collaboration, and which I thought had some chance of being produced as an *X-*

Files episode. I couldn't have been more wrong in the latter instance. I was very naive about how Hollywood works. The only reason that Brandon Trenz and I wrote a movie adaptation of "Harlequin" was that the story had been optioned by David Lynch's production company The Picture Factory. It was pure coincidence that this came not long after we had written the *X-Files* episode. If we hadn't already gotten some scriptwriting experience doing that, we would never have tried to write a spec script for "Harlequin." And unless you're into screenwriting for the long haul, you're not going to make that much money.

TW: I have a crazy wish: a *Simpsons* episode witten by Thomas Ligotti.

Ligotti: Yes, that is a crazy wish. Actually, there is a remote connection between my horror stories and *The Simpsons*. One of my all-time favorite guitar players, Danny Gatton, did a cover version of *The Simpsons* theme song on his first major-label album. A few years later, Gatton killed himself just as *The Agonizing Resurrection of Victor Frankenstein* was in production. I dedicated that book to the memory of Danny Gatton, who I always thought was just a normal, happy guy, aside from being a genius guitar player.

TW: Please imagine the preposterous situation of hosting a TV talkshow. You could invite three guests. Whom would you choose (including dead persons)?

Ligotti: The first person that comes to mind is Ronald Reagan, addled with Alzheimer's and now crippled with a broken hip. I don't think I'd need any other guests if I could get Reagan. But I'd also like a syphillis-ravaged Al Capone as my co-host. And for the band . . . Jimi Hendrix playing his feedback-drenched rendition of the Star-Spangled Banner throughout the entirety of the show.

EMA: One of your favourite actors is Udo Kier. He once said, "They say that Hollywood movies have no soul. I sometimes think that European movies have too much soul." Would you also accept this statement for European horror stories?

Ligotti: I understand Udo Kier's quote to mean that Europe has produced a lot of slow and boring movies, which I would agree with. Same goes for Japan, in my Ugly American opinion. If you don't include England as part of Europe, which I don't, then I can't think of very many European writers who wrote horror stories strictly speaking. I once bought an English translation of a collection of stories and poems by a Czech horror writer who had recently killed himself. I thought to myself, "This is going to be great." Unfortunately the most obvious influence on this writer's work were old episodes of *The Twilight Zone.* I wish there were translations of more European horror writers. Writers like Bruno Schulz, Dino Buzzati, and the Hungarian writer Geza Csath I don't consider horror writers but genuinely literary writers. The same would apply to the stories of Georg Heym, even though at least one of them, "The Autopsy," has appeared in horror anthologies. Loosely speaking, I would agree that the work of these writers does have more "soul" than American or British horror fiction, but this is a quality much more suited to literature than to movies. There is an person behind a literary work, a soul if you like. There isn't any such thing in movies, where so many people are involved.

TW: Let's return to merciless reality. Even if this may sound unpopular: I think that it is a cruel fate to be forced to work for other people, dictated by the need to earn one's living. The modern civilized human spends more time at his working place than at home. Problems at work haunt us even in our spare time, thus killing even more life time off. . . . Imagination, creativity and even common sense suffer from this fact. In this context, I have very much enjoyed your new stories "I Have A Special Plan For This World" and "My Work Is Not Yet Done" (both are going to appear in 2002 in your new book *My Work Is Not Yet Done: Three Tales of Corporate Horror,* Mythos Books, Missouri,   http://www.bibliocity.com/   home/mythosbooks). Would you say that you share my repulsion concerning work and working situations?

Ligotti: In the United States a person isn't required to answer questions that might incriminate him. But I would like to point out that in the stories to which you refer, there are only provisional good guys and bad guys. Ultimately everyone in those stories is bad news, as is the entire human race in my view. And, most importantly, those stories only begin with horrors in a workplace setting. Ultimately they are about something else altogether.

EMA: Your "Corporate Horror Stories" are different from what we know from your earlier works. Your style has changed quite a bit, if I'm permitted to say so. They are located in "normal" surroundings and the characters live through "normal" things (normal only to a certain degree). What was the cause for this radical change of style?

Ligotti: Actually, the only story that's relatively normal is the title novella. That was dictated by plot of the story, and also by the fact that I originally thought of that story as a movie.

EMA: Once you told me that you're not interested in Science Fiction. How come that you chose an SF scenario for "The Nightmare Network" (also appearing in *My Work Is Not Yet Done: Three Tales of Corporate Horror)*?

Ligotti: That story was modelled after the writings of Burroughs, who is the king of the sort of twisted, apocalyptic scenarios that are essential to "The Nightmare Network." Given the Burroughs influence, I knew that I would need to write some gruesome ideas and images into that story, and my usual style would simply not accommodate these narrative elements.

TW: On the threshold to the 20th century, the so-called Millennium horror has been very successful—a play with the fears of modern, civilized humans facing a new era when everything might as well be destroyed. . . . It seems that this trend didn't influence you. Doesn't Thomas Ligotti believe in the near apocalypse?

Ligotti: No, of course not. That would be insane to believe such a thing.

TW: What does religion mean to you?

Ligotti: Crowd control.

TW: . . . Politics?

Ligotti: Also crowd control.

TW: . . . Psychology?

Ligotti: Control on the level of the individual. Freud and Jung type psychology is patently insane nonsense, although relatively few people are subject to its control. I prefer psycho-pharmacology, even if the potential for control is far more extensive that "talking therapies."

TW: . . . Drugs?

Ligotti: Like everything else in this world, they're more trouble than they're worth. But if I hadn't cracked up back in 1970 I'd probably still be a drug-hog.

TW: . . . Are there any things you are afraid of? Do you know "angst"?

Ligotti: You're kidding, right? I'm afraid of *everything*. I'm even afraid of betraying specific things that I'm afraid of.

EMA: In your introduction to *The Nightmare Factory,* "The Consolations of Horror," you wrote: "In other words, you get the horrors you deserve." Do you think that you, yourself, deserve the horrors you experience?

Ligotti: The reference, I believe, was to horrors in fiction. As for real life, there is no deserving or not deserving, just as there are no values, no morals, no rights, none of that rhetorical debris that makes our lives a misery far beyond that ordained by the facts of our physcial existence.

EMA: Which human qualities do you like most? And which ones do you loathe most?

Ligotti: I'm like everyone else. I like people who are most like I am. I dislike people who are least like I am.

EMA: If you had a wish to make for the future, what would you desire most?

Ligotti: I don't even have to think about this one. Here's my wish: That every living thing, at the moment of its death, expires in a state of bliss. All's well that end's well. Of course this would upset the natural order of things, and people would be killing themselves left and right. In order to insure the continuation of this funhouse of flesh that we call Life, it's necessary that we fear the pain and grief of death and at all costs struggle to avoid the inevitable.

TW/EMA: Finally we'd like to quote you: "My outlook is that it's a damn shame that organic life ever developed on this or any other planet . . ." (from the interview with Robert Bee). Is Thomas Ligotti a nihilist? Do you dream of an anorganic black nothingness—the purity of an absolute void? Do you dream of your own "Tsalal" (Tsalal is the Hebrew word for the conception of all-consuming darkness)?

Ligotti: Well, "all-consuming darkness" kind of suggests that there's something going on in the universe. That's not what I would wish. I don't want a universe in which even nothing could be going on.

TW/EMA: Thank you, Mr. Ligotti, it was very kind of you to reply to our questions.

THE TRANSITION FROM LITERARY HORROR TO EXISTENTIAL NIGHTMARE IN THOMAS LIGOTTI'S "NETHESCURIAL"

Matt Cardin

Thomas Ligotti's "Nethescurial" can be classed with a half-dozen or so of his tales which deal directly with a theme that is never absent from his fiction, but which he sometimes approaches more obliquely than others: the theme of transcendent, mystical, ontologically absolute evil. Of particular interest in this story is the way Ligotti augments its emotional power through his use of rich descriptive language and, most importantly, through the use of metafictionally-flavored multiple framing devices to create the sense of the literary-existential barrier being breached.

"Nethescurial," which can be found in Ligotti's collection titled *Grimscribe: His Lives and Works,* is framed as a letter or journal written by a man (or perhaps a woman; the sex of the narrator is never specified) who has stumbled across a previously unknown late nineteenth-century manuscript in a library archive. The manuscript relates the story of an ancient religious sect devoted to an evil god, and by the end of "Nethescurial" the narrator discovers that the merely literary horror of the tale in the manuscript has overtaken his own existential reality.

The story is told in three sections. The first, titled "The Idol and the Island," describes the discovery of the manuscript and summarizes its contents in some detail. According to the narrator, the manuscript seems to be a letter, or perhaps a journal entry, written by one Bartholomew Gray (a self-admitted alias) and relating the story of Gray's visit to "an obscure island located at some unspecified northern latitude" at the request of an anthropologist referred to only as Dr. N—. When Mr. Gray arrives, he observes that the very structure of the island and its fauna appear to have been twisted or mutated into a sort of nightmarish aspect. Dr. N— reveals to Mr. Gray that he (Dr. N—) has found buried on the island a fragment of an ancient religious idol whose worshippers had apparently held the pantheistic belief that "all created things—appearances to the contrary—are of a single, unified, and transcendent stuff, an emanation of a central creative force." The faith of these people was shattered when "one day it was revealed to them, in a manner both obscure and hideous, that the power to which they bowed was essentially evil in character and that their religious mode of pantheism was in truth a kind of pandemonism." They coined the name "Nethescurial" to reflect the evil character of the force they served, and then they destroyed their idol and dispersed its fragments to various secret locations around the world. Despite their efforts to destroy the cult, there survived a sect which remained devoted to the service of Nethescurial, and Dr. N— speculates that perhaps he and Mr. Gray are in danger from this very sect. In a plot twist that is expectable (according to the narrator who is summarizing this manuscript), it turns out that Mr. Gray is himself one of the surviving servants of Nethescurial, and that he has in fact brought with him to the island the other collected fragments of the idol. He takes the last fragment from Dr. N— by force and then sacrifices the unfortunate anthropologist to the god, but later he repents of his evil deed after encountering some "horrific surprises," and finally he manages to make his escape from the island, throwing the pieces of the idol into the ocean in the process. The manuscript purports to be his own account of the matter.

The narrator of "Nethescurial" casts some aspersions on the literary style of this old manuscript, calling it somewhat incoherent, formulaic, and poorly developed, but he then admits that the central idea of pandemonism is "intriguing," and he reveals a certain latent fascination in his own self with the kind of horror described by the story. The section ends with the narrator mentioning in a jocular tone that it is time for him to go to bed.

The second section of the story, titled "Postscript," is dated "Later the same night," and is penned by the narrator while he is still suffering the aftereffects of a horrific nightmare. In the nightmare he had found himself on the isle of Nethescurial, where he witnessed the ritual (and willing) sacrifice of a worshipper to the god. The overwhelming sense of horror and panic that could only be hinted at by the manuscript was communicated to him vividly in the dream. He felt menaced by "an unseen presence, something I could feel was circulating within all things and unifying them in an infinitely extensive body of evil." Perhaps worst of all, he could also feel this evil presence "emerging in myself, growing stronger behind this living face that I am afraid to confront in a mirror." He concludes his remarks with the thought that he will surely be back to normal by morning.

In the third section, titled "The Puppets in the Park" and dated "Some days later, and quite late at night," the narrator notes that his own continuing letter (which of course forms the body of the story) "has mutated into a chronicle of my adventures Nethescurialian." He is awash in horror: unable to take nourishment, and compelled to wear gloves and keep moving because of the nightmarish presence he sees "squirming" and "gushing" inside all things, he has begun to hear an ominous chant sounding from the subconscious minds of everyone with whom he comes in contact. He makes his way to an outdoor park at night, where he stumbles across a puppet show in a clearing. At some point during the show, the puppets freeze and slowly turn to look directly into his eyes. He is standing behind the back row of the audience, and suddenly he notices that the audience members are looking at him as well: they are all turned around on their benches and staring at him "with expressionless faces and dead puppet eyes." He hears a silent chant sounding from their subconscious minds, a chant about the omnipresence of a certain evil entity—the same chant, in fact, that appears in the manuscript about the isle of Nethescurial—and he eventually returns home. Once there he burns the manuscript in his fireplace, but the smoke seems unwilling to rise up the chimney, preferring instead to hang above the smoldering ashes in a cloud of mutating and suggestively horrible shapes. The tale ends with the narrator trying to convince himself that reality is not what he has come to fear, that "*Nethescurial is not the secret name of the creation,*" and finally that "I am not dying in a nightmare."

The emotional and psychological impact of this tale is quite profound, as many readers can attest. As stated in the introduction, two of the most important factors in creating this effect, aside from the sheer potency of the story's central theme, are Ligotti's rich descriptive language and his clever use of multiple framing devices. For the first part, Ligotti invests his story from the beginning with an aura of cosmic strangeness when he "quotes" the chant at the beginning of the fictional manuscript: "In the rooms of houses and beyond their walls—beneath dark waters and across moonlit skies—below earth mound and above mountain peak—in northern leaf and southern flower—inside each star and the voids between them—within blood and bone, through all souls and spirits—among the watchful winds of this and the several worlds—behind the faces of the living and the dead . . ." The evocative tone of this passage sets up an expectation of weirdness and profundity that is amply sustained by the rest of the story. Employing a technique borrowed from Poe, Ligotti alternates these poetically-toned passages with more mundane ones, such as the narrator's flippant remarks about the inherent weaknesses of horror stories. At the end of the story when the narrator suddenly lapses into florid, adjective-loaded language to speak of his impending personal apocalypse (and perhaps of the universal one?), the effect is truly unnerving:

> See, there is no shape in the fireplace. The smoke is gone, gone up the chimney and out into the sky. And there is nothing in the sky, nothing I can see through the window. There is the moon, of course, high and round. But no shadow falls across the moon, no churning chaos of smoke that chokes the frail order of the earth, no shifting cloud of nightmares enveloping moons and suns and stars. It is not a squirming, creeping, smearing shape I see upon the moon, not the shape of a great deformed crab scuttling out of the black oceans of infinity and invading the island of the moon, crawling with its innumerable bodies upon all the spinning islands of inky space. That shape is not the cancerous totality of all creatures, not the oozing ichor that flows within all things. Nethescurial is not the secret name of the creation.

Of course, Ligotti is working at the same disadvantage that plagues any writer of fiction who wants his work to have a real impact on the reader: a story is just a story, and it will never be "real life" in the same sense as the reader's own immediate subjective experience. This is precisely why Ligotti's use of framing devices is so important to "Nethescurial's" overall effect: the technique calls attention to the reader's relationship to the ontological world of the story. "Nethescurial" contains four narrative levels: first, the story of the ancient cult of Nethescurial as related by Dr. N—; second, the story of Dr. N— and "Bartholomew Gray" as penned by Mr. Gray; third, the story of the narrator as told through his letter (which, as mentioned above, makes up the body of "Nethescurial"); and fourth, the story of the narrator's letter itself, i.e. the unspoken context of the very story the reader is reading. Each successive level frames the previous ones. Dr. N— tells Mr. Gray the story of the ancient cult; the narrator reads of Dr. N— and Mr. Gray in Gray's manuscript; and the reader encounters the narrator's thoughts in a "letter" which is actually the story itself. This very structure calls attention to the fact of the reader's status as a reader, which in turn lends extra power to Ligotti's tactic of breaching the narrative levels. Level one (the ancient cult) breaches level two (Dr. N— and Mr. Gray) when Mr. Gray turns out to be a member of the cult and murders Dr. N—. This level in turn breaches level three (the narrator) when he is apparently overtaken by the evil god described in the manuscript. If we ask about the breach of the fourth level by the third—that is, of the reader's world by the story "Nethescurial" itself—we can only say that this of course cannot be accomplished directly, since that would entail the reader's existential world being transformed into the story world. But then, *that is exactly what Ligotti is writing about.* He seems almost to be playing a game with the reader's sense of distance from the horrors of the story. For example, he quite deliberately has the unnamed narrator comment on the literary qualities of the newly-discovered manuscript, which of course creates a sense of distance between the two (manuscript and narrator). He even has the narrator reflect upon the inability of supernatural literature to effect a real belief on the part of the reader: "The problem," the narrator writes, "is that such supernatural inventions are indeed quite difficult to imagine. So often they fail to materialize in the mind, to take on a mental texture, and thus remain unfelt as anything but an abstract monster of metaphysics—an elegant or awkward schematic that cannot rise from the paper to touch us" (81-2). Ligotti even has the narrator take a kind of comfort in this distance: "Of course, we do need to keep a certain distance from such specters as Nethescurial, but this is usually provided by the medium of words as such, which ensnare all kinds of fantastic creatures before they can tear us body and soul" (p. 82). The trick comes in when, as we have already seen, the narrator's sense of safety with his narrative distance from the manuscript is proved to be ill-founded. The analogy between this situation and the reader's own relation to the story is surely a significant factor in "Nethescurial's" emotional impact.

In a comment about H.P. Lovecraft's "The Colour out of Space" in her introduction to *American Gothic Tales*, Joyce Carol Oates notes that the story represents "the wholly obverse vision of American destiny; the repudiation of American-Transcendentalist optimism, in which the individual is somehow divine, or shares in nature's divinity. In the gothic imagination there has been a profound and irrevocable split between mankind and nature in the romantic sense, and a tragic division between what we wish to know and what may be staring us in the face." In "Nethescurial" and other stories, Thomas Ligotti has taken this technique to a new level: he posits the *truth* of the Transcendentalist doctrine of ultimate unity, but then raises the question: What if this unity is not blissful, but nightmarish? What if the god who is our very self turns out to be a monster? In Ligotti's fictional world, the answer to this question lies all around us and within us. We cannot escape from the nightmare when the nightmare turns out to be our own soul.

WORKS CITED

Ligotti, Thomas. *Grimscribe: His Lives and Works*. New York: Jove Books, 1994.

Oates, Joyce Carol. *American Gothic Tales*. New York: Plume, 1996.

THE DARK BEAUTY OF UNHEARD-OF HORRORS

Thomas Ligotti

It is not necessary, perhaps not even possible, for a story to mean just what it says. Beneath the surface utterances of setting, incident, and character, there is another voice that may speak of something more than the bare elements of narrative. The things this other voice has to express must be interpreted for the mind through the strictly conspicuous aspects of the story, though such interpretations are often wildly various. (Religious parables offer the most obvious example of this chaotic phenomenon.) In greater accord, one hopes, are the emotions experienced in the course of reading, since emotion, not mind, is the faculty for hearing the secret voice of the story and apprehending its meaning. Without emotion, neither story nor anything else can convey meaning as such, only data. This, not entirely original, argument goes double, if not more, for stories of the supernatural.

More than many other types of stories, it is crucial that those of the supernatural make their statement of meaning as much as possible by means of emotion, especially the present advanced stage in the development of this literary genre. Years of exegesis have made interpreting supernatural tales into a game that anyone can play, and one finds that gods and demons are quite easily relocated from the dreams in which they were born into some mundane context of sociology, psychology, politics, or whatever. The result is pathetic and, in the worst sense of the word, grotesque. One of the noblest and most tragic figures of the imagination was the vampire—damn his soul, and our own. But to see this marvelous, terrifying creature reduced to a plastic Halloween mask for sexual or political repression has been a tedious outrage. The vampire attained his stature through the emotion of fear of a fantastic evil, yet how utterly he has lost it all at the heavy, hammering hands of explication. Rest in peace, Nosferatu, none will ever take your place.

If the vampire no longer raises the emotion he once did, perhaps it is partly his own fault. He lost his mystery because he had so little of it to start. His nature and habits were always documented in detail, his ways and means a matter of public record. Too many laws lorded over him, and all laws belong to the natural world. Like his colleague the werewolf, he was too much a known quantity. His was a familiar, most of the time human body, and it was used like a whore by writers whose concerns were predominantly for the body as well as the everyday path in which it walks. Consequently, the vampire was stripped of all that made him alien to our ordinary selves, until he was transformed into merely the bad boy next door. He remained a menace, to be sure, but his focus shifted from the soul to the senses. This is how it is when a mysterious force is embodied in a human body, or in any form that is too well fixed. And a mystery explained is one robbed of its power of emotion, dwindling into a parcel of information, a tissue of rules and statistics without meaning in themselves.

Of course, mystery actually requires a measure of the concrete if it is to be perceived at all; otherwise is only a void, the void. The thinnest mixture of this mortar, I suppose, is contained in that most basic source of mystery—darkness. Very difficult to domesticate this phenomenon, to collar it and give a name to the fear it inspires. As a verse writer once said:

> *The blackness at the bottom of a well*
> *May bold most any kind of hell.*

The dark, indeed, phenomenon possessing the maximum of mystery, the one most resistant to the taming of the mind and most resonant with emotions and meanings of a highly complex and subtle type. It is also extremely abstract as a provenance for supernatural horror, an elusive prodigy whose potential for fear may slip through a writer's fingers and right past even a sensitive reader of terror tales. Obviously it is problematic in a way that a solid pair of gleaming fangs at a victim's neck is not. Hence, darkness itself is rarely used in a story as the central incarnation of the supernatural, though it often serves in a supporting role as an element of atmosphere, an extension of more concrete phenomena. The shadowy ambiance of a fictional locale almost always resolves itself into an apparition of substance, a threat with a name, if not a full blown history. Darkness may also perform in a strictly symbolic capacity, representing the abyss at the core of any genuine tale of mystery and horror. But to draw a reader's attention to this abyss, this unnameable hell of blackness, is usually sacrificed in favor of focusing on some tangible dread pressing against the body of everyday life. From these facts may be derived an ad hoc taxonomy for dividing supernatural stories into types, or rather a spectrum of types: on the one side, those that tend to emphasize the surface manifestations of a supernatural phenomenon; on the other, those that reach toward the dark core of mystery in purest and most abstract condition. The former stories show us the bodies, big as life, of the demonic tribe of spooks, vampires, and other assorted bogeymen; the latter suggest to us the essence, far bigger than life, of that dark universal terror beyond naming which is the matrix for all other terrors. Prominent among the last-named tales is H. P. Lovecraft's "The Music of Erich Zann."

II

The most radical form of the unknown, and the least adulterated avatar of mystery, darkness is all-pervasive in "The Music of Erich Zann.' In addition to functioning as a natural atmospheric element in the tale, it is ultimately revealed as the primary supernatural phenomenon. The story reaches its pitch of uncanny revelation when the narrator witnesses "the blackness of space illimitable" in place of the reassuring city lights he expected to see through the window of Erich Zann's garrett room. There are only two things we can know about this mysterious blackness: first, that in some indefinable way it is both menacing and alluring (a usual, perhaps necessary conjunction in horror tales); second, that it has an important, and once indefinable, connection with Erich Zann and the strange music he plays on a viol. Zann is portrayed as a musician of genius, yet he performs with a "cheap theatre orchestra" and resides in a freakishly dilapidated boarding house in the, also freakishly dilapidated, Rue d'Auseil. He himself is described as being physically and psychically deformed in such a way that identifies him with the Rue d'Auseil and its crooked, leaning houses. This is his realm, which may be prison or paradise or both, and with his death at the end of the story it disappears from this earth, if it ever was in fact on it. Indeed, neither Zann nor the street was ever part of material reality, for Zann's world "lay in some far cosmos of the imagination." It is to this world that the narrator is unaccountably drawn at the beginning of the story and which he also seeks to recover after he flees the "marvels and terrors" introduced to him by the bizarre German musician.

Just as there exists an intimate correspondence between Zann and the Rue d'Auseil, and between Zann's music and the blackness beyond the wall the summit of that unreal street, there is also an identification between Zann and the narrator. Both of them are victims of "hysical and nervous suffering." More significantly, they are each in thrall to the "dread of vague wonder and brooding mystery" of an unearthly music and by extension to the dark doom that this music seems both to conjure and to keep at bay. Earlier in the story, the narrator makes an effort to whistle some of the "weird notes" he has heard Zann playing in his crummy garrett room, an act that seems to stir up certain forces beyond the room's window; later, Zann plays these same notes as if they had some power against the advancing blackness. Perhaps that power is one of both invocation and exorcism allowing Zann to play with another power, namely that of a supernatural music-maker who produces "shriller, steadier note" than Zann's, "a calm, deliberate, *purposeful, mocking* note from far away in the West." (Italics mine: apparently at the time this story was written, 1921, Lovecraft did not yet perceive the alien forces of the universe as "indifferent," nor had he begun to anthropomorphize them that culminated in the Old Ones of "At the Mountains of Madness," who are called "men" for all their superficial strangeness.) What led Zann into this terrible duet with the dark is unknown, though his perpetuation of this relationship is characterized as something of a vice by the narrator, who observes the performing Zann "dripping with perspiration and twisted like a monkey" and who impressionistically symbolizes Zann's music with visions of "shadowy satyrs and Bacchanals dancing and whirling insanely & through seething abysses of clouds and smoke and lightning."

Certainly Zann is aware of the temptations of his music, and does his best—or does he?to quell the curiosity it has aroused in the narrator. But the exact nature of Zann's obsession is left in darkness—the "notes" the Old German composes in explanation of himself, unlike Alhazred's *Necronomicon*, would have been far too unearthly and alien to simple human feeling to survive even in fragments; hence, they are wisely lost to the world. What brought this man "who signed his name as Erich Zann"—as if he had another name, or perhaps none—to that run-down boarding house in the Rue d'Auseil? What caused him to remain on that twisted street? Above all, what is it about the blackness and its "shocking music" that so possesses him? (Of course, the identical questions might be asked concerning the narrator, who is in a position to inform us of the answers but, for obscure reasons unable to.) Interestingly lucid is the fact that the supernatural aspect of the story—that reverberant blackness which threatens to overwhelm the city beyond Zann's window and possibly the entire world—is exclusive to Zann, and, by some occult transference or predisposition, the narrator. After the narrator flees the Rue d'Auseil, he finds that the rest of the city has been unaffected by the fantastic cataclysm that occurred in his old neighborhood. But, as previously established, Zann and the Rue d'Auseil were, at the very least, sympathetic entities, a district unto themselves—and when he disappeared into the blackness he seems to have taken the street, which was as old and misshapen as he, along with him.

In the blackness is the secret core of the primary supernatural phenomenon of the story, whereas Zann's music may be viewed as an ancillary phenomenon, a more credible and tangible quality that allows one to grasp, however tenuously, the utterly mysterious. And in the blackness the mystery must remain, nameless and unknown, leaving only the memory of a certain haunting music to suggest, as subtly as possible, its meaning. It is the abstract, elusive form of supernatural horror in this story that may account for its enduring enchantment for certain readers.

"The Music of Erich Zann" was Lovecraft's early, almost premature expression of his ideal as a writer: the use of maximum suggestion and minimal explanation to evoke a sense of supernatural terrors and wonders. It is also among those of his stories that bear the greatest resemblance to the masterpieces Lovecraft most admired and held as touchstones for excellence in the realm of the weird: Blackwood's "The Willows," Machen's "The White People," Poe's "Fall of the House of Usher." Like those tales, "The Music of Erich Zann" ultimately withholds its secrets and preserves its mystery; narrative gives a peculiar shape to perennial enigmas, creating a new landscape at the center of which is the same ancient abyss (and outside of which is the void). Later, in "The Colour out of Space," Lovecraft fashioned a visual counterpart to the aural mysteries of "The Music of Erich Zann," a pernicious and inexplicable entity that arrives from the black well of the cosmos to blacken the life of our earth. No surprise that Lovecraft conjoined these two tales as his best, setting them apart from those of the famous Cthulhu Mythos which, by contrast, seem to fall into the category of "explained" supernatural fiction after the manner of Ann Radcliffe. In the earlier story as much as the later one, that secret voice beneath the narrative speaks strongly and stridently, imparting its meaning through feelings rather than facts, singing a song without words on the theme of the nameless horror and strangeness of the universe, that cosmic neighborhood where everything that is, is terrifyingly wrong . . . and at the same time alluring, a place of charming evil.

"The Music of Erich Zann" seems to say: stay away from the Rue d'Auseil. In actuality, however, it invites us to make our home there, haunts us, as the narrator of the story is haunted, and inspires us to find again something that was lost, to seek out that blackness and play to it at our peril . . . without ever knowing why. This is a familiar experience for those "sensitive few" whose responses form the foundation of Lovecraft's aesthetic of supernatural horror. Illuminating this ordeal which is indulged in for its own sake by aesthetes of the unknown, Jorge Luis Borges has written: "Music, states of happiness, mythology, faces molded by time, certain twilights and certain places—all these are trying to tell us something; that imminence of a revelation that is not yet produced is, perhaps, the aesthetic reality."

The above quotation cannot fail to remind us of so many statements made by Lovecraft concerning those sensations which, as he asserted, alone made his existence endurable. Among such declarations is the following: "Sometimes I stumble accidentally on rare combinations of slope, curved street-line, roofs & gables & chimneys, & accessory details of verdure & background, which in the magic of late afternoon assume a mystic majesty & exotic significance beyond the power of words to describe . . . All that to capture some fragment of this hidden & unreachable beauty; this beauty which is all of dream, yet which I have known closely & reveled in through long aeons before my birth or the birth of this or of any other world."

In "The Music of Erich Zann," Lovecraft captured at least a fragment of the desired object and delivered it to his readers. Like Erich Zann's "world of beauty," Lovecraft's "lay in some far cosmos of the imagination," and like that of another artist, it is a "beauty that hath horror in it."

LIMINAL TERROR AND COLLECTIVE IDENTITY IN THOMAS LIGOTTI'S "THE SHADOW AT THE BOTTOM OF THE WORLD"

Matt Cardin

But I wanted to witness what could never be
I wanted to see what could not be seen—
The moment of consummate disaster
When puppets turn to face the puppetmaster.
        —Thomas Ligotti, "I Have a Special Plan for This World"

Thomas Ligotti is arguably the preëminent living writer of horror fiction. This critical reputation has grown up around him over a period of twenty years, during which time he has remained paradoxically obscure in the mainstream literary consciousness, and even, astonishingly, among some segments of horror fandom. Ligotti has long been known for the extreme darkness of his philosophical vision, and in this paper I shall examine this darkness as it relates to his story "The Shadow at the Bottom of the World," which can be found in his collection *Grimscribe: His Lives and Works,* as well as in his omnibus collection titled *The Nightmare Factory.* Specifically, I shall examine the ways in which the story uses the motifs of liminal terror and collective identity to achieve the acme of philosophical nightmarishness that readeres have come to recognize as the hallmark of Ligotti's fictional *oeuvre.*

PLOT SUMMARY

"The Shadow at the Bottom of the World" relates the story of an unspecified rural town which experiences an unnatural prolongation of the autumn season one year. The sights, sounds, and smells of autumn ripen to an almost unbearable pitch, until one night the town's residents see a scarecrow begin to move in a grotesque fashion in a farmer's field on the edge of town. They gather the next day to examine the scarecrow, and when they attack it and remove its outer garments, they discover not the expected wooden frame but "something black and twisted into the form of a man, something that seemed to have come up from the earth and grown over the wooden planks like a dark fungus, consuming the structure" (Ligotti, *Grimscribe*, p. 222). In a vague communal panic, they dig deep into the earth to find the base of the stalk, but no matter how far they dig, they cannot find its end. By the next day the stalk has disappeared ("It's gone back," says the farmer who owns the field. "Gone into the earth like something hiding in its shell" (224)), and in its place there is now a wide and seemingly bottomless pit. The overripe autumn season continues to linger over the following days and weeks until eventually the townspeople's dreams are affected. "In sleep," they say,

> we were consumed by the feverish life of the earth, cast among a ripe, fairly rotting world of strange growth and transformation. We took a place within a darkly flourishing landscape where even the air was ripened into ruddy hues and everything wore the wrinkled grimace of decay, the mottled complexion of old flesh. The face of the land itself was knotted with so many other faces, ones that were corrupted by vile impulses. Grotesque expressions were molding themselves into the darkish grooves of ancient bark and the whorls of withered leaf; pulpy, misshapen features peered out of damp furrows; and the crisp skin of stalks and dead seeds split into a multitude of crooked smiles. All was a freakish mask painted with russet, rashy colors—colors that bled with a virulent intensity, so rich and vibrant that things trembled with their own ripeness. But despite this gross palpability, there remained something spectral at the heart of these dreams. It moved in shadow, a presence that was in the world of solid forms but not of it. Nor did it belong to any other world that could be named, unless it was to that realm which is suggested to us by an autumn night when fields lay ragged in moonlight and some wild spirit has entered into things, a great aberration sprouting forth from a chasm of moist and fertile shadows, a hollow-eyed howling malignity rising to present itself to the cold emptiness of space and the pale gaze of the moon. (p. 225-6)

Things come to a head one night when two strangers, a woman and a small boy, arrive in town unexpectedly and begin to walk the streets. The townspeople watch from their windows as one of their own named Mr. Marble goes out to meet them. Mr. Marble is an old eccentric, well known to everyone, who all along has seemed to understand much more about what is happening than the other townspeople are able to grasp. He is a blade sharpener by trade, an "old visionary who sharpened knives and axes and curving scythes" (p. 227), and the spell of the season seems to have overtaken him with an especially virulent intensity. On the night of the visitors' arrival, he reappears from an unexplained absence and begins to stalk the streets with a blade in his hand: "Possessed by the ecstasies of a dark festival, he moved in a trance, bearing in his hand that great ceremonial knife whose keen edge flashed a thousand glittering dreams" (p. 228). The townspeople watch in anticipation as he approaches the visitors to perform the rightful sacrifice that will culminate the energies of this aberrant season. But his hand trembles; he is unable to do it, and the woman and the boy flee. The next morning the townspeople find him facedown in the farmer's field, dead of a self-inflicted wound from his own blade. His blood appears to be of the same substance that grew up from the ground and into the scarecrow, and they take the body and throw it into the pit.

COLLAPSING CATEGORIES

From the outset, "The Shadow at the Bottom of the World" abounds in details that invite the reader to analyze the story in terms of the motif of liminality. By this term I refer to the idea, so familiar to poststructuralist critics, of a state or category that does not conform to the rigidly defined distinctions of conventional thinking, but instead falls somehow "between" the lines of generally accepted categories. The term "liminal" is borrowed from the discipline of anthropology, where many investigators have used it to refer to the status of tribal members during the period of their initiation into full adulthood. Such people are regularly viewed as neither adults nor children for the duration of the initiation ceremony, and as such they "elude or slip through the network of classifications that normally locate states and positions in cultural space" (Turner, p. 95). In a word, they are *liminal* entities.

The significance of this idea for the current paper can be found in the fact that encounters with liminal phenomena almost always produce a sense of strangeness, uncomfortableness, or uncanniness. This reaction accounts for the fact, noted by structuralist theorist Edmund Leach, that "whenever we make category distinctions within a unified field . . . it is the boundaries that matter; we concentrate our attention on the differences, not the similarities, and this makes us feel that the markers of such boundaries are of special value, 'sacred', 'taboo'" (Leach, p. 35). This is so, simply because an encounter with something that falls on the interstices of one's conceptual and cultural "world" tends to remind one of the fact that virtual mountains of phenomena have been, and are being, excluded from one's field of vision by the classificatory grid itself. One realizes that reality itself is much bigger and stranger and more unbounded than one usually perceives it to be, and thus the validity of the grid is called into question. Sociologist Peter Berger argues that "the socially constructed world is, above all, an ordering of experience. A meaningful order, or nomos, is imposed upon the discrete experiences and meanings of individuals" (Berger, p. 19). Berger further argues that nomization is every society's most important function. To be separated from the nomizing influence of society, he says, is to be in danger of experiencing a sense of meaninglessness, which in his view is "the nightmare *par excellence*, in which the individual is submerged in a world of disorder, senselessness and madness. Reality and identity are malignantly transformed into meaningless figures of horror. To be in society is to be 'sane' precisely in the sense of being shielded from the ultimate 'insanity' of such anomic terror" (p. 22).

The question at hand, of course, is whether such an experience of anomic terror (which for the purposes of this paper shall be equated with *liminal* terror) is possible without being separated from a societal nomos. Is it possible that hints of this terror may filter into the daylight world of nomic reality through the interstices of the classificatory grid (which in structural terms would be explained as a system of binary opposites) that define the world's parameters? Is it possible that literature might serve as one such venue for the experience of liminal terror? Literary critic Scott

Carpenter points out that the use of literary techniques that emphasize the fuzzy boundaries between our conceptual categories—that is, techniques which emphasize the *limen*, the threshold between the categories—"traditionally excite[s] the fear and fascination of readers. Thus the intersection of such opposites as living/dead gives rise to ghost stories (phantoms being both animate and inanimate), the blending of human and inhuman gives birth to such figures as Frankenstein's monster, and the intermingling of past and present becomes the stuff of science fiction." He continues with the sociological observation that "Historically, elements corresponding to the logic of both/and are regarded by society as exceptional, scandalous, and even monstrous. Often efforts are made to repress or at least to neutralize these representations of 'in-between-ness'" (Carpenter, p. 60).

Quite clearly, the experience of liminal terror can indeed be generated by literature, and this brings us back to Ligotti's "The Shadow at the Bottom of the World." As mentioned above, the story seems almost to invite the reader to analyze it in terms of its use of the motif of liminality, and this gives us a clue about the ways in which the story will attempt to affect its readers. Consider, for example, the second sentence of the first paragraph, in which the narrator says that the strange mood of the prolonged autumnal season was evident to everyone, "whether we happened to live in town or somewhere outside its limits" (Ligotti, *Grimscribe*, p. 219). The liminality of the space between town and countryside is a common theme in some anthropological literature. This is a slippery space: where exactly does town become country? When you find yourself on the outskirts of a town, how can you know for sure whether you are located inside or outside its limit? Immediately, Ligotti has called attention to this liminal space, and has thus begun to invest the story with a mood of liminal terror.

The same issue is brought out even more clearly in the next sentence: "(And traveling between town and countryside was Mr. Marble, who had been studying the seasonal signs far longer and in greater depth than we, disclosing prophecies that no one would credit at the time.)" (p. 219) The liminal space that was referred to only obliquely in the previous sentence is now made explicit. Notice that Mr. Marble's liminal status—he travels "between town and countryside"—is reinforced by the fact that the sentence is enclosed in parentheses. In a way, it can be said that we put mental "parentheses" around all liminal phenomena by relegating them to the periphery of our attention, and so the sentence in which we first meet Mr. Marble has the double effect of situating him in liminal space both in content and in form. This interpretation gains added weight from the fact that the second mention of him in the story, two paragraphs later, is also parenthetical: "But everything upon that land seemed unwilling to support our hunger for revelation, and our congregation was lost in fidgeting bemusement. (With the exception, of course, of Mr. Marble, whose eyes, we recall, were gleaming with illuminations he could not offer us in any words we would understand.)" (p. 221)

In the second paragraph of the story, the narrator describes a field that lies "adjacent to the edge of town," providing yet another invocation of the liminal space between town and countryside (p. 220). The strange nocturnal dance of the scarecrow represents yet another instance of liminality. What is it about scarecrows that seems so strange to so many people? Why do scarecrows sometimes appear as prominent figures in weird literature and horror movies? One reason may be that scarecrows are effigies of the human form, and as such they call attention to another basic category distinction, the distinction between human and not-human. (At this point the reader is referred to Ligotti's longtime fascination with dolls and dummies.)   On a subconscious level, scarecrows seem to resist being neatly categorized as either completely human (since they are not alive) or completely non-human (since they are vaguely man-shaped), and so they provoke a peculiar emotional reaction, namely, the experience of liminal terror. When a scarecrow is portrayed as standing alone in a field on a breezeless night, and then beginning to kick its legs as it raises its face to the moonlit sky, one may easily imagine the heightening of the effect that results.

On the morning after the nocturnal dance of the scarecrow, when the townspeople arrive at the farmer's field, things seem rather dreamy and murky. It almost seems as if the people are unable to fully wake up: "The sky had hidden itself behind a leaden vault of clouds, depriving us of the crucial element of pure sunlight which we needed to fully burn off the misty dreams of the past night" (p. 221). This passage highlights yet another basic category distinction: the line between waking reality and dreaming reality. In the famous words of the Chinese sage Chuang Tzu, "Are you a man who dreamed you were a butterfly, or are you now a butterfly dreaming that you are a man?" Strictly speaking, in subjective experience it is impossible to answer this question either way with complete confidence. Equally impossible is the attempt to remember the precise moment when one crosses over from wakefulness into sleep, or vice versa. The very fact that our lives are divided into two realms of consciousness whose fuzzy boundaries make them anything but discrete provides fertile ground for the experience of liminal terror.[1] In "The Shadow at the Bottom of the World," this truth is exploited by the inability of the narrator to fully wake up on the morning following the scarecrow's dance. Henceforth, the very narration itself can be viewed as taking place in the liminal space between waking and dreaming, and the fact that the story is narrated in the first person means that the reader experiences his or her own reading self as being located in the same space.

There is a symmetry in the story's use of liminal periods of time. As with sleep and waking, so with night and day: when exactly does one become the other? Twilight and dawn can both be seen as liminal periods. Significantly, the attack of the townspeople on the scarecrow occurs at twilight, and when they gather back at the field the next morning, it is at the precise moment when "the frigid aurora of dawn appeared over the distant woods" (p. 224).

Near the story's midpoint, the literary cues encouraging us to interpret the story in terms of the experience of liminal terror begin to increase in scope. When the townspeople begin to have their vivid dreams of "a ripe, fairly rotting world of strange growth and transformation," they are beginning to see the dissolution of all their conceptual and perceptual categories. When the visions from their dreams—the faces and figures visible on walls, the overripe colors of the leaves, etc.—begin to make their appearance in waking reality itself, it is apparent that the "other world" glimpsed in liminal spaces is on the verge of breaking through and overrunning the daylight world of conceptual categories. The concluding sentence of this section explicitly describes a liminal presence, an unknown and unknowable something that exists not in the categories of our world (or any other) but *between* them, and is thus worth quoting again:

> It moved in shadow, a presence that was in the world of solid forms but not of it. Nor did it belong to any other world that could be named, unless it was that realm which is suggested to us by an autumn night when fields lay ragged in moonlight and some wild spirit has entered into things, a great aberration sprouting forth from a chasm of moist and fertile shadows, a hollow-eyed howling malignity rising to present itself to the cold emptiness of space and the pale gaze of the moon. (pp. 225-6)

This is the closest the story gets to describing the nature of the reality which seems to be pressing in upon the daylight "world of solid forms," and the reality so described would seem to correspond in every respect to Berger's description of anomic reality as "a world of disorder, senselessness, and madness" in which "reality and identity are malignantly transformed into meaningless figures of horror" (Berger, p. 22).

More than any other single element, the fact that the story is set in an extended autumn season serves to invest it with a sense of liminal strangeness and terror. During the spring and summer, the world is alive. During the winter it is dead. During autumn it is both, and neither. Of course, the boundaries between all seasons are indistinct, but with autumn the sense of strangeness seems to be particularly pronounced. It is no accident that Halloween, the holiday devoted to acknowledging and celebrating the dark side of life, occurs during this season. Ligotti himself speculates about this quintessential mood of autumn in the opening paragraph of the story when he describes the common thread winding its way through all the autumn scenes pictured on all the calendars in the homes of the townspeople:

> On the calendars which hung in so many of our homes, the monthly photograph illustrated the spirit of the numbered days below it: sheaves of cornstalks standing brownish and brittle in a

newly harvested field, a narrow house and wide barn in the background, a sky of empty light above, and fiery leafage frolicking about the edges of the scene. But something dark, something abysmal always finds its way into the bland beauty of such pictures, something that usually holds itself in abeyance, some entwining presence that we always know is there. (Ligotti, *Grimscribe*, p. 219)

This "entwining presence" is none other than the liminal strangeness that seems to be more palpable during the autumn months than at any other time of the year. In the very next sentence, the narrator announces this autumn weirdness as the very subject of the story: "And it was exactly this presence that had gone into crisis. . . ."[2]

The liminal strangeness of autumn is also accented in this story by the fact that for some reason, autumn won't end. Winter will not come. The temporal setting becomes more and more strange, more and more liminal, as the leaves that should have fallen long ago remain on the trees, and as the field that should have frozen long ago remains warm. As mentioned above, autumn is already a liminal season. The end of autumn is even more so, and Ligotti prolongs this end until the story seems to take place in a time that nobody has ever known before, a time that is familiar and yet unfamiliar, beautiful yet hideous, flourishing yet decaying. Above all, it is a time that is thoroughly terrifying in its liminality.

THE MANY IN THE ONE

This investigation of the liminal motif in "The Shadow at the Bottom of the World" does not deliver its full reward until we consider it in light of the second motif I have chosen to emphasize, which is the motif of collective identity. We can see at a glance that the story is told in the first person plural. The pronoun I does not appear a single time. Instead, the townspeople seem to narrate the story with a single voice (all emphases in the following quotes are mine): "The field allowed full view of itself from so many of *our* windows" (p. 220). "Soft lights shone through curtained windows along the length of each street, where *our* trim wooden homes seemed as small as dollhouses beneath the dark rustling depths of the season" (p. 224). "*Our* speculations were brief and useless" (p. 224). "It was not long after this troubling episode that *our* dreams, which formerly had been the merest shadows and glimpses, swelled into full phase" (p. 225). "But the truth is that we wanted something to happen to them—we wanted to see them silenced. Such was our desire" (p. 229). This narrative voice, while relatively rare, is hardly unheard of in the annals of literature, but in this particular story it is unusually important, and we will find that a careful consideration of it will elicit some significant points.

For instance, consider for a moment the first person plural narrative voice in light of the concept of liminal terror as developed in the paper up to this point. Viewed this way, we immediately begin to sense the strangeness of the voice. In concrete reality we never experience a communal voice either objectively or subjectively (the claims of Freudian psychoanalytic theory about repression etc. notwithstanding). In fact, in concrete reality we never experience such a thing as a *group*. Consider, for example, the idea of "fruit." You cannot hold "fruit" in your hand. "Fruit" is a category, a conceptual grouping that is useful for purposes of classification and recognition, but that in truth has no concrete referent. In existential reality you can only hold a specific fruit, e.g. an apple or a banana. The same is true of human groupings. There is no such existential entity as a group, e.g. a town. There is real land, there are real houses and streets and street lamps, there are real individual people, but the grouping of these separate entities into the collective entity known as a "town" is a conceptual exercise, and this leads us to view the first person plural narrative voice as something extremely peculiar, something that tends to inspire feelings of liminal terror and strangeness. The collective narrator of "The Shadow at the Bottom of the World" can exist only in mental space. Even if a thousand people were to read the story aloud in unison, they would still amount to nothing more than a thousand separate voices. At no point could we say that a true collective voice had emerged from the group reading. Ligotti's use of the collective narrator immediately creates an aura of otherworldly strangeness; as we read the story we are placed inside the mind of an entity that is at once entirely familiar (the population of a town) and yet entirely strange (the collective voice of a town).

Having established this point, it becomes most interesting and revealing to note the use of the third person to refer to characters in the story, because such instances serve to sharpen the boundaries of the collective narrator's identity. There are only five people in the story who are referred to in the third person: Mr. Marble, the farmer who owns the field containing the scarecrow, the anonymous townsperson who says "Maybe there'll be some change in the spring" (although this person may still be considered to exist within the boundaries of the collective narrator), and the woman and child who arrive in town unexpectedly. Whenever someone is referred to in the third person, he or she is thereby placed outside the boundary of the "we" who are telling the story. The logic behind these instances seems to make sense. The farmer owns the field from which the black stalk erupts, and the collective narrator wants to distance him/her/itself from the strange manifestation. The farmer is excluded from the boundary of the narrator's collective identity simply by virtue of the fact that he is too closely associated with something the narrator fears. The person who speaks of a possible change in the spring may still be considered a member of the group; perhaps "someone said" may be taken as implying "one of us said." The mother and son are complete outsiders; their very alienness to the narrator seems to bring out the narrator's greatest fear: "Our fear was what they might have known, what they must certainly have discovered, about *us*" (p. 229, Ligotti's emphasis).

But these instances are all overshadowed by the extended treatment of Mr. Marble, who possesses by far the strongest individual identity of any character in the story. He is always referred to in the third person, and interestingly, his notable individuality seems to be bound up somehow with the fact of his liminal positioning. He is notable because he travels "between town and countryside" both physically and in his thoughts. His deep knowledge makes him opaque: his "eyes, we recall, were gleaming with illuminations he could not offer us in any words we would understand." He is able to "read in the leaves" the activities of that strange liminal presence that is forcing its way into the light. The fact that he sharpens blades for a living only serves to reinforce his individuality and his liminal status: blades cut, blades separate, just as the sharpness of Mr. Marble's mind slices through, and perhaps widens, the lines or cracks in the world through which the liminal presence is emerging. Importantly, he is the only character in the story to be given a separate name, and the name "Marble" itself suggests the streaking or mottling of separate colors (read: separate conceptual categories) that would occur if the liminal were transposed with the conceptual or the nomic.

Ironically—or perhaps all too expectedly—Mr. Marble's individuality, his ability to see and think on his own apart from the crowd, renders him especially susceptible to assault and domination by the invading presence. His mental acuity fades as he is drawn further and further into the thrall of the dark presence, until eventually he is entirely under its control, much in the manner of the scarecrow, which was invaded by the "thick dark stalk which rose out of the earth and reached into the effigy like a hand into a puppet" (p. 222). Before being taken over by the presence, Mr. Marble unwittingly states his own doom as a cryptic prophecy: "Doesn't have arms, but it knows how to use them. Doesn't have a face, but it knows where to find one" (p. 227). When the strangers arrive in town on the night when the gathering eruption is obviously coming to a head, the liminal has become central. After having been referred to twice in parentheses, after having spent so much time "traveling between town and countryside," Mr. Marble is now at the center of the town and the center of events. In the mind of the collective narrator, by all rights Mr. Marble should kill the visitors. This is the end toward which the entire upsurge of energy has been leading. The proper sacrifice will signal the completion of the strange mutation. The energy has reached a peak and must be discharged.

But at this point the story reveals an even deeper layer, a layer that further complicates the issue of collective identity vs. individual identity, and that promises to bear fruit in our ongoing investigation of the story's use of liminal terror. Even though Mr. Marble's "outsideness," his liminality and individuality, are responsible for opening him up to control by the invading presence, they also endow him with the freedom to choose. When he chooses not to complete the sacrifice, and instead to vent the gathering energy on himself, the true heart of the narrator's identity is revealed by the fact that they want the sacrifice to be completed. They want the outsiders to be killed because "only then would we be sure that they could not tell what they knew. . . . Our fear was what they might have known, what they must certainly have discovered, about us."

Which one has truly surrendered self-control to the invading dark presence, Mr. Marble or the narrator? Mr. Marble can still resist. The townspeople cannot, because—and here is the awaited reward—*they realize that the nightmarish reality attempting to break through into their daylit world is none other than their own deepest self.* The dark thing is the root of their own collective identity. It is they who have been controlled by the black stalk rising up into the scarecrow "like a hand into a puppet." The very fact that they have been speaking in a collective voice, which, as noted above, can occur only in a liminal space, shows that this dark root has been behind their thoughts and actions all along. Their horror is *self* horror. They do not want to become self-conscious, to recognize and know the horrible thing which they are.

THE VOICE OF OUR NAME

Although "The Shadow at the Bottom of the World" was originally published in issue number sixteen of the British horror magazine *Fear*, we can deepen our understanding of its secrets by viewing it as being organically related to Ligotti's second collection of short stories, titled *Grimscribe: His Lives and Works,* in which it is the final piece. This allows us to relate it back to the framing device Ligotti introduces at the beginning of the book, where in the introduction the stories in the collection are framed as tales told by a metaphysical entity who has no name, but who for the purposes of the book has decided to call itself Grimscribe. It is also said that his name is the name of everyone, and that "he keeps his name secret, his many names. He hides each one from all the others, so that they will not become lost among themselves. Protecting his life from all his lives, from the memory of so many lives, he hides behind the mask of anonymity" (Ligotti, *Grimscribe,* ix). This could just as well be taken as describing the narrator of "The Shadow at the Bottom of the World," a story which is appropriately the only entry in the final section of the book titled "The Voice of Our [i.e. Grimscribe's] Name" (other sections being titled "The Voice of the Damned," "The Voice of the Demon," "The Voice of the Dreamer," and "The Voice of the Child"). Considered in light of Grimscribe as a whole, this story may be viewed as being narrated by Grimscribe itself in the first person, standing out at last from behind the mask of the other characters in whose guises it has appeared (all the stories in *Grimscribe* are told in the first person). If Grimscribe is indeed the name of everyone, then the near transposition of worlds in "The Shadow at the Bottom of the World" represents the near loss of all sanity and identity. The collective identity of the town brings about the horror, because such collectivity is already the beginning of that "backward slide," as Grimscribe calls it, "into that great blackness in which all names [i.e. identities] have their source" (ix).

The narrator's (Grimscribe's) fear of what the visitors might have discovered about it may arise at least in part from the fact that the discovery of the townspeople's secret is also the discovery of the visitors' secret. That is, the madness passes itself on through the recognition of one's own secret self in another. Grimscribe's careful self-deception almost comes unraveled in a horrible birth of self-awareness. When Grimscribe/the townspeople drop Mr. Marble's body into the bottomless pit, its/their motives are obscure. On the one hand, they are still horrified by the black substance that has replaced Mr. Marble's blood, and this shows that they are still horrified at the possible discovery of their own identity. On the other hand, they envy and hate Mr. Marble because he represents the individuality which eludes them. The key to understanding their action lies in the recognition that in a perverse way, they/Grimscribe wanted their own destruction to be complete. The murder of the outsiders would have killed the spread of the townspeople's self-knowledge, but it would also have signaled the successful conquest of the daylight world by the darkness, and thus brought an end (albeit not a pleasant one) to their, and Grimscribe's, torturous charade. Grimscribe would have met the darkness and discovered it to be his own self, and there would have been no one left to say or do or know or suffer or fear or be anything. But since the rightful sacrifice was aborted, Grimscribe must continue the charade, and conscious beings must continue to suffer the ambivalence of simultaneously fearing and longing for ultimate self-knowledge, until at last, in the words of Ligotti's prose poem "Primordial Loathing," "that perfect lid of darkness falls over this world once more" (*Noctuary* 179).

NOTES:

1. Cf. Berger, pp. 42-3: "It would be erroneous to think of these situations [in which the reality of everyday life is put into question] as being rare. On the contrary, every individual passes through such a situation every twenty hours or so—in the experience of sleep and, very importantly, in the transition stages between sleep and wakefulness. In the world of dreams the reality of everyday life is definitely left behind. In the transition stages of falling asleep and waking up again the contours of everyday reality are, at the least, less firm than in the state of fully awake consciousness. The reality of everyday life, therefore, is continuously surrounded by a penumbra of vastly different realities. These, to be sure, are segregated in consciousness as having a special cognitive status (in the consciousness of modern man, a lesser one) and thus generally prevented from massively threatening the primary reality of fully awake existence. Even then, however, the 'dikes' of everyday reality are not always impermeable to the invasion of those other realities that insinuate themselves into consciousness during sleep. There are always the 'nightmares' that continue to haunt in the daytime—specifically, with the 'nightmarish' thought that daytime reality may not be what it purports to be, that behind it lurks a totally different reality that may have as much validity, that indeed world and self may ultimately be something quite different from what they are defined to be by the society in which one lives one's daytime existence."

2. As one might guess from his deeply emotional description of the season, autumn is Ligotti's favorite time of year, and "The Shadow at the Bottom of the World" is his favorite among his own works for precisely this reason. "Autumn has always held a special magic for me," he has said, "and I tried to put as much of that feeling as I could into this story" (Paul & Schurholz, 20).

WORKS CITED:

Berger, Peter L. *The Sacred Canopy: Elements of a Sociological Theory of Religion.* New York: Doubleday, 1967.

Carpenter, Scott. *Reading Lessons: An Introduction to Theory.* Upper Saddle River, NJ: Prentice-Hall, 2000.

Leach, Edmund. *Culture and Communication: The Logic by Which Symbols Are Connected.* Cambridge: Cambridge UP, 1976.

Ligotti, Thomas. *Grimscribe: His Lives and Works. New York: Jove Books, 1994.*

_____. *Noctuary.* New York: Carroll & Graf, 1994.

Paul, R.F. and Keith Schurholz. "Triangulating the Daemon: An Interview with Thomas Ligotti." *Esoterra* #8 (Winter/Spring 1999): 14-21.

Turner, Victor. The Ritual Process: Structure and Anti-Structure. New York: Aldine de Gruyter, 1995.

TWILIGHT TWILIGHT NIHIL NIHIL: THOMAS LIGOTTI AND THE POST-INDUSTRIAL ENGLISH UNDERGROUND

William Burns

"For anyone who has an interest in the work I have created with Current 93 over the last thirteen years, I *must* say: Read Ligotti."
—David Tibet, 1996

"What I like most about Current 93's work is its sheer visionary intensity, and what I like to consider is its morbidity and world-disgust."
—Thomas Ligotti, 1999

In the works of Thomas Ligotti, music is not a primary image or metaphor, and yet his themes of alienation, dissonance, and the ecstasy of nothingness have made Ligotti a co-conspirator with English "outsider" artists such as Current 93, Coil, and Nurse with Wound. For Ligotti, silence is a much more ubiquitous and revelatory sound; in Ligotti's universe, the nullifying silence of existence is deafening to its all too human inhabitants. The only overt literary use of music by Ligotti is in "The Music of the Moon" from 1989's *Songs of a Dead Dreamer* (an insightful title for a collection of short stories, equating prose and ballad). Much like Lovecraft's "The Music of Erich Zann," "The Music of the Moon" utilizes a dizzying overture as a vehicle to altered consciousness; the listener becomes immersed and entangled in the jarring yet hypnotic ambience of pure sound: "Music and silence became confused, indistinguishable from each other, as colors merge into whiteness." This pandemonic drone, reflecting the chaos and ominous babel permeating the fabric of the universe, reverberates through the compositions and ideological perspectives of the leading visionaries of the English post-Industrial underground.

Thomas Ligotti's tastes in music are not exactly avant-garde: surf music and instrumental rock bands such as The Shadows, The Merman, Pell Mell, and The Aqua Velvets as well as guitar virtuosos such as Eric Johnson, Steve Morse, and Danny Gatton[1]. If it were not for the efforts of Current 93's David Tibet, it is entirely possible that Ligotti would not have had any knowledge of "England's hidden reverse," the post-Industrial movement's experimental and oracular investigations into art, magic, spirituality, and sexuality. Tibet, having discovered *Songs of a Dead Dreamer*, sensed a kindred shadow in Ligotti, writing to him and sending Ligotti the entire Current 93 catalogue. From this auspicious beginning, a tenebrous relationship was born, spawning both musical and literary projects, which would involve many of post-Industrial's prominent figures. To understand and appreciate why Ligotti's works and (anti-) world view would appeal to and inspire such singular personalities, it might be helpful to review the genesis of such an influential yet obscured cultural movement.

The post-Industrial crusade emerged from the twisted shrapnel of Industrial culture. The initial Industrial bands[2], Throbbing Gristle, Cabaret Voltaire, SPK, and artists like San Fran madman Monte Cazazza, took the rage and subversiveness of punk rock and funneled them through the death factories of Auschwitz, the war mechanisms of Vietnam, and the killing fields of Cambodia.[3] A reaction to the failure of the English Labour revolution and the rise of Thatcherism in the late 70s and early 80s, Industrial bands explored the late capitalist technological holocaust: noise, the abject, transgressive information exchanges, conspicuous consumerism, and nuclear Armageddon. Music was DIY propaganda trying to dismantle or infect systems of control and conformity, deconstructing the rock star as God, career path Pornography, serial murders, Fluxus art in opposition, self-mutilating Aktionists, CIA covert ops, Futurism, William S. Burroughs, assembly-line electro pop, and anatomical aberrations were all ground up in the Industrial infernal machine. Extending the disillusionment with '60s ideals[4], Industrial "musicians" were alienated from all institutions, most of all from notions of humanity and human progress.

With the termination of Throbbing Gristle in 1981, the post-

Industrial movement rose like a mushroom cloud. The fallout from Throbbing Gristle created two bands consisting of its former members: Chris and Cosey and Psychic TV. Joining Genesis P. Orridge and Peter Christopherson in Psychic TV were converts like David Tibet and John Balance. These sonic dissectionists would collaborate in various projects leading to the emergence of Current 93 (Tibet) and Coil (Balance and Christopherson) and the eminence of Steven Stapleton and his dada-esque Nurse with Wound. Post-Industrial musicians were more willing to incorporate various musical genres and sound sources into their agendas than their progenitors and were less political and more philosophical, mystical, and aesthetically open, retreating from global and media concerns to a personal, inwardly directed alchemic quest for enlightenment. The occult, esoteric, and pagan corners of British history are their focus as romantic archetypes of beauty and decay are revealed as two sides of the same cosmic coin. Art-music-ritual represents the decadent stream that unites all the eccentric travelers along the hidden temporal pathways of England. Obviously, this fascination with the nocturnal, the autumnal, and the chaotic would find both its scribe and muse in the form of Thomas Ligotti.

The first sprouting of the post-Industrial/Ligotti flowers of evil occurred on Current 93's 1996 release *All the Pretty Horses (The Inmost Light)* (Durtro 30)[5]. Tibet's form of "apocalyptic folk and menstrual minstrels" presents Nature as an anarchic force with the power to create and destroy with little rhyme or reason, indifferent to the fears and desires of human beings. Within this tumultuous existence, the notion of childhood innocence as a redemptive escape into a fantastic world, an act of desperation to pre-empt the sad, bleak world of adulthood, is Tibet's thematic focus on *All the Pretty Horses*. Tibet's lyrics are often poetic invocations of eschatology, a radiant annihilation that causes humans to question their own relationship to and readiness to face the splendor and awe of the infinite. For Tibet, the lyrical content of his songs is not as important as the tone and totality of effect produced for the listener, much like the atmospheric absorption of Ligotti's work, especially in his prose poems.

The first explicit reference to Ligotti on *All the Pretty Horses* is "The Frolic," taking its title and its looming dread from Ligotti's short story "The Frolic" from *Songs of a Dead Dreamer*[6]. Tibet takes the listener into the menacing reveries of Ligotti's playful predator: "What is that that lies? / Deadchilddead / I have such nightmares and you're all in them / It's worse than you or I can ever know."

Using looped child voices, Tibet and his musical translators Steven Stapleton and Michael Cashmore create a haunting fairy tale, a singsong sketch of malevolent innocence. "Twilight Twilight Nihil Nihil (for Thomas Ligotti who has seen the bloodbells shine)" is an obvious paean to the author, a truly horrid composition using disturbing sounds to surround John Balance's intonations: "Who will deliver me from this body of death?" and the answer "Nihil." While this "song" reflects the despairing emptiness of Ligotti's fictional worlds, Tibet's own beliefs seem to be in opposition to this hopeless situation. The subtitle of *All the Pretty Horses*, the *Inmost Light*, represents Tibet's view that there is an inherent transcendent "joy" that illuminates the Savior within all human beings. Tibet's appreciation of Ligotti may be more of an aesthetic and affective esteem rather than a strict philosophical or metaphysical agreement. That said, Ligotti's nihilistic estrangement contaminates almost all of *All the Pretty Horses*, even those tracks that do not explicitly reference Ligotti like "The Carnival is Dead and Gone" and "The Long Shadows Fall." Ligotti even has the last words on the album. Following "Patripassian," Ligotti, recorded over the phone, reads the poem that ends his short story "Les Fleurs" from *Songs of a Dead Dreamer*, which mentions Tibet's beloved feline friends:

> *To Eden with me you will not leave*
> *To live in my cottage of crazy crooked eaves.*
> *In your own happy home you take care these nights;*
> *When you let your little cat in, turn on the lights!*
> *Something scurries behind and finds a cozy place to stare,*
> *Something sent to you from paradise, paradisically so rare:*
> *Tongues flowering; they leap out laughing, lapping. Disappear!*

All the Pretty Horses is a work that negotiates the tensions of hope and despondency felt by humanity in the face of our own mortality.

The next Ligotti/Tibet synthesis was a true meeting of the minds: a book and accompanying CD, limited to 2,000 copies (since reissued in an unlimited form with altered packaging), with artwork by Steven Stapleton. *In a Foreign Town, In a Foreign Land* (Durtro 35), a reference to Current 93's "Falling Back in Fields of Rape" from *Dogs Blood Rising,* was released in 1997, consisting of four interrelated short stories with corresponding soundtracks for each story. Words and music merge perfectly on this work, as Tibet, Stapleton, and Christoph Heeman's cacophonous mélange of manipulated sounds become an actual character adding to the lurid taint of Ligotti's setting. Ligotti seems to be very conscious of the project's literary and musical confluences as three of the titles of his stories ("The bells will sound forever," "A soft voice whispers nothing," and "When you hear the singing, you will know it is time") implicate sound and tonality as sinister ingredients in the nightmarish landscape. Ligotti's psychogeography conflates space, structure, and inhabitants sharing the same essence, alignments that all intersect and feed one deranged transubstantiation:

> Even in a northern border town of such intensely chaotic oddity and corruption there was still some greater chaos, some deeper insanity, than one had counted on, or could ever be taken into account—wherever there was anything; there would be chaos and insanity to such a degree that one could never come to terms with it, and it was only a matter of time before your world, whatever you thought it to be, was undermined if not completely overrun, by another world.

This all-consuming delirium is signaled by Tibet's use of layered schizoid voices and the numbing chimes of bells signaling an equinox of the void. *In a Foreign Town, In a Foreign Land* not only represents the first of a series of fruitful collaborations but also inaugurated Ligotti's work for Durtro Press, Tibet's publishing company dedicated to Decadent and macabre authors such as Count Stenbock and David Barnitz.

Ligotti would act solely as a stimulus for Current 93's 1998 *Soft Black Stars* (Durtro 42), a much more stark and minimalist work utilizing Tibet's voice and a piano with the barest accompaniment of strings and woodwinds. The title of the album comes from a frighteningly beautiful image from Ligotti's "Teatro Grottesco" (*The Nightmare Factory*), a short story that equates artistic impulses with expungement and expurgation. *Soft Black Stars* is an introspective catharsis as if the Inmost Light is flickering and shrinking in the darkness: "the empty streets / the songs of twilight / the clouds at rest / the church bells chiming / a scarecrow shudders and songbirds tremble / I looked at you and saw it's time." On *Soft Black Stars*, Ligotti's northern border town has become completely internalized; the end comes not even with a whimper but in unnerving silence.

The year 2000 brought with it a unique work of millennial madness: Ligotti and Current 93's *I Have a Special Plan for this World* (Durtro 48). Based on a series of discorporeal prose poems (published by Durtro Press in an edition of 125 copies) by Ligotti and cassette tapes made by a bizarre stranger encountered by Ligotti through his job in Detroit (also the source material for Ligotti's "The Bungalow House" from *The Nightmare Factory*), *I Have a Special Plan for this World* is a return to the extended sound collaging of *In a Foreign Town, In a Foreign Land*, merging the reality of dreams and the urgency of nightmares as revealed through the psychotic ramblings of "Bungalow Bill" (the name Tibet gave the speaker on the original "Bungalow House" tapes). Interestingly, Ligotti's short story "I Have a Special Plan for this World" has little convergence with this project except for the title and a harrowing insight into a rationally deranged mind. Individually, both poems and music have a startling power, yet Ligotti's apocalyptic poesy does not completely gel with Tibet's unhinged composition with the same morbid intensity that *In a Foreign Town, In a Foreign Land* exudes. The 12" vinyl release of *I Have a Special Plan for this World* contains a slightly different mix of Tibet and Stapleton's work but, more importantly, contains unmanipulated excerpts from the original "Bungalow House" tapes on the flip side, seriously disturbing monologues that are only hinted at by the samples used on the clamorous titular product.

In August of 2000, Tibet suffered a particularly Ligottiean experience. Much like the narrator of "Teatro Grottesco," Tibet was hospitalized with intense abdominal pain, caused by appendicitis, and the delirious Tibet saw Blakean visions of angels, psychopomps, and helicopters leading to a revelation about the "Soul of Man" and the "Four Last Things." This prophetic encounter with the infinite produced two works in which Tibet attempts to reconcile his near death experience with his creative instincts: *The Great in the Small* (Durtro 53) and *Purtle* (UDOR 8), a joint release with Nurse with Wound. Perhaps unconsciously, Tibet has internalized the Ligottian motif of illness and contagion as reflecting the artistic impulse: the artist as a host for a virus-like corruption that causes the body to reject itself in the form of a creative work[7].

2001's *This Degenerate Little Town* (Durtro 66) is the project that seems to reflect the mutual respect and inspiration between Tibet and Ligotti most equally. Like their previous two collaborative works, *This Degenerate Little Town* (both book and CD limited to 160 copies) consists of a Ligotti authored text and a CD containing a musical backdrop created by Tibet and Stapleton to enhance Ligotti's own readings of his poetic pieces. Managing to incorporate the mapping of the empty contours of the soul from *In a Foreign Town, In a Foreign Land* and the nihilistically obsessed mania of *I Have a Special Plan for this World*, *This Degenerate Little Town* is Ligotti's most concentrated expression of the putrification infesting existence. Tibet and Stapleton's accompanying music is simplicity itself: reverberating, melancholic tones elevating Ligotti's stately delivery to a sinister grandeur. Tibet has promised a more expansive "paramusical dreamscape" based on Ligotti's poems for the future.

Although David Tibet is the artist with the most specific references to the works of Thomas Ligotti, the incestuous nature of the English post-Industrial underground makes it entirely possible that Ligotti has affected Tibet's peers. John Balance has been a frequent guest on Current 93's releases, and his own musical project Coil reflects many Ligottiean interests: physical metamorphosis, Dionysian frenzy, sadism, and the magical periphery. Coil's *Musick to Play in the Dark 1* (1999) and *2* (2000) are atmospheric manifestations of psychic collapse and spiritual debasement. Steven Stapleton has been lauded by Tibet since their first meeting in

1983 and has contributed to every Current 93 release. Stapleton's Nurse with Wound revels in obtuse moods and dark surrealism, and his damaged artwork (whether painting, sculpture, or collage) is what Ligotti's fictional artists would create if they were real (God help us).

Thomas Ligotti's relationship with the post-Industrial English underground seems to be one of fellow artistic explorers deviating from mainstream conceptions of literature and music. All of these artists attempt the transmutation of binary oppositions that are taken as being natural and absolute: good and evil, life and death, spirituality and physicality, civilization and primitivism. The reciprocal nature of the projects creates a network of influence that asks the reader and listener to not except the world as it is, to see our existence as askew, and to appropriate a mindset that might not be as comforting, secure, or simple as we have been taught. It must be somewhat reassuring for Thomas Ligotti to realize that those individuals who stare into the abyss are not as alone as his works suggest and that the painful, nullifying realizations of life might be creatively promising.

SOURCES:

Current 93. *All the Pretty Horses (The Inmost Light)*. Durtro 30. 1996.

Current 93 with Thomas Ligotti. *In a Foreign Town, In a Foreign Land*. Durtro 35. 1997.

Current 93. *Soft Black Stars*. Durtro 42. 1998.

Current 93. *I Have a Special Plan for this World*. Durtro 48. 2000.

Current 93/Nurse with Wound. *Purtle*. UDOR 8. 2001.

Current 93. *This Degenerate Little Town*. Durtro 66. 2001.

Keenan, David. "From a Lonely Place." *The Wire*. Issue 160, June 1997. 26-30.

Keenan, David. "Childhood's End." *The Wire*. Issue 163, September 1997. 34-37.

Keenan, David. "Time Out of Joint." *The Wire*. Issue 175, September 1998. 48-53.

Ligotti, Thomas. *Songs of a Dead Dreamer*. New York: Carrol & Graf, 1989.

Ligotti, Thomas. *The Nightmare Factory*. New York: Carrol & Graf, 1996.

Ligotti, Thomas. *In a Foreign Town, In a Foreign Land*. London: Durtro, 1997.

Ligotti, Thomas. I *Have a Special Plan for this World*. London: Durtro, 2000.

Ligotti, Thomas. *This Degenerate Little Town*. London: Durtro, 2001.

Ligotti, Thomas. "Obsession Always Leads to Fear: An Interview with David Tibet of Current 03." *Esoterra*. Issue 8, Winter/Spring 1999. 26-29.

Paul, R.F. and Keith Schurholz. "Triangulating the Demon: An Interview with Thomas Ligotti." *Esoterra*. Issue 8, Winter/Spring 1999. 14-21.

Tibet, David. "Interview with Thomas Ligotti." *Aklo*. Eds. Mark Valentine, Roger Dobson, and R.B. Russell. Oxford: Tartarus Press/Caermaen Books, 1998. 160-163.

The author would like to thank Gil Gershman for his assistance.

NOTES:

1. Ligotti dedicated his collection *The Agonizing Resurrection of Victor Frankenstein* to Gatton's memory.

2. The term "Industrial" to designate these bands and artists was suggested by Monte Cazazza's slogan "Industrial Music for Industrial People" and Throbbing Gristle's record label Industrial Records.

3. Steven Stapleton's Nurse with Wound released their first album *Chance Meeting on a Dissecting Table of a Sewing Machine and an Umbrella* (1977) only a few months after Throbbing Gristle's epochal *Second Annual Report,* chronologically placing Nurse with Wound in the early stages of the Industrial movement and yet Stapleton has vehemently dismissed this categorization, insisting his music be designated as "surrealist."

4. Ligotti has also related his own disheartening and unsatisfying experiences with the spiritual aftermath of the transcendental philosophies of the 1960s.

5. This full scale assault was heralded in 1995 with Current 93's 12"/CDEP *Where the Long Shadows Fall (Before the Inmost Light)* (Durtro 28) where fifteen seconds of "The Frolic" was previewed as an addendum. The 1998 compilation *Foxtrot* (a benefit album to help pay for John Balance's alcohol rehabilitation) contained a remix of "The Innermost Light Itself" enti-

tled "A Dream of the Inmost Light" which credits Ligotti with "Hawaiian Plucked Steel." More of Ligotti's musical abilities are promised to be showcased by Tibet on CD in the future.

6. In 1997, Current 93 contributed a song to the World Serpent compilation *Terra Serpentes* entitled "Frolicking." Unfortunately, the author has not heard this piece and cannot say conclusively that this is another Ligotti-inspired composition but the title is suggestive of a Ligotti connection.

7. This theme can be seen in "Teatro Grottesco" and "Severini" from *The Nightmare Factory* and "The Shadow, the Darkness" in the anthology *999*.

SOFT BLACK STAR: SOME THOUGHTS ON KNOWING TOM LIGOTTI.

David Tibet

I loved, when I was younger, a song called "Darkness, Darkness." Recently, when I started my yearly spiralling back to childhood thought and teenage dreaming, I bought the new Robert Plant album, *Dreamland*. And I found there the same song, a cover of Jesse Colin Young's beautiful and melancholy ballad. I again immersed myself in that familiar and comforting shadow, the snow, the past. The formless beauty that comes with unshaped fears, as we track the thunder and lightning whilst sitting safe inside, the fire burning, the clock chiming smilingly. The sound of stars flying into infinity, and comets crashing, watched in widescreen, unreal, a play, a film, a game. Youth flies to cosy darkness. In horror literature, this can be found best represented—this comfortable unease—in the works of M.R. James.

Ligotti, however, breathes the air of another ethical and spiritual universe altogether. Like many other readers, my initial encounter with his work and his world was with the Robinson paperback edition of *Songs of a Dead Dreamer*, the expanded and revised version of the Silver Scarab edition of the same title. The first story in this collection is "The Frolic." I was terribly disturbed by it, to the degree that I was unsure as to whether to read any more of the book. It repelled me. Fittingly, a story so stilted and dreamlike began to invade my own dreams. I found it difficult to pick up the book again—it frightened me very much—and I left it on a desk for some weeks, all the time thinking of those words of such strangely beautiful terror: *"for in the black-foaming gutters and back alleys of paradise, in the dank windowless gloom of some galactic cellar, in the hollow pearly whorls found in sewerlike seas, in starless cities of insanity, and in their slums . . . my awe-struck little deer and I have gone frolicking. . . ."* I think this is perhaps the most apocalyptic passage in horror ever written, equalled only by the entirety of Thomas de Quincey's *Suspiria de Profundis*, and, despite any protestations Tom Ligotti might have to the contrary, the banality of its fear, the squalid and stupid realism of that terror that permeates those words he wrote is far more un-nerving to me than all of Lovecraft's idiot gods and horrific mani-festations from the cosmic depths. In this sad and sick world in which we routinely hear of the existence of child-murderers like the Belgian sado-paedophile Marc Dutroux, and disgusting kill-ings such as those of two young girls in the small English town of Soham, those words of Tom's seem prophetic, and so true to the ugly and unhappy litany of life in these decadent and degenerate end-times. Every time I re-read Tom's work, I am left wondering how anyone can have crafted something so individual and utterly alone, and so true to life, despite its unimaginative filing in the fantasy sections of the bookshop and catalogue.

My nature is obsessive. This manifests in the usual way, in my trying to collect everything by and about those I admire, so I can be with them and walk with them in their strange and unique land. Most of the objects of my obsessions are deceased. But with those artists whom I admire and who still live, my real aim is to get to know them, so I can be part of their world, and see, at least temporarily, through their visionary eyes. I obtained Ligotti's home address through my friend Andy Richards of Cold Tonnage Books, and sent him an admiring letter with a large selection of my albums. While I no longer have a copy of the letter, I recall that I told him that I thought he and I shared a similar view of the world and its heart, though we had drawn different conclusions. Both Tom and I saw a fallen world, but I believe in redemption. Tom had gone to that terrible place beyond worlds, beyond re-demptions, beyond words, where even the silence was ferocious and painful. Nonetheless I wanted to work with him, and know him, very badly indeed. Having kept all of the many hundreds of e-mail letters between Tom and myself, I see that my first letters to him cover Tiny Tim (and the rumour that Jim Carrey was to make a film about his life), decadent literature, the making of the Cur-rent 93 album *All the Pretty Little Horses* (which I then described to him as "a Current 93 album sung entirely in Gregorian Chant"), and comments made by my friend Timothy d'Arch Smith—re-nowned historian of occult literature and late 19th century homo-sexual verse (who first introduced me to the works of Count

Stenbock) and rare bookseller without equal—concerning the Golden Dawn and the secret sister organisation he claimed existed for catamites everywhere, the Golden Down.

Tom once wrote to me that he was working towards achieving an effect in his prose style that would make his stories read as if they had been awkwardly translated from some Eastern European language into English. It impressed me enormously; he had struck exactly on that mélange of menace and paranoia inadequately decorated with a slight layer of forced charm that characterises a whole genre of translation, where the threat of that strange force which strives to destroy our souls is masked as a quirky visitation of fate upon the smug world of the *petit bourgeois* (the stories of Stefan Grabinski may serve as an example of this phenomenon). Yet Tom has at times also claimed that he is absolutely in the tradition of HP Lovecraft, and that HPL remains for him his biggest influence and the greatest visionary in the world of the fantastic story.

Though Lovecraft's importance cannot be denied, I see Ligotti's work as far more dreamlike, far more terrifying. His prose style has never struck me as anything less than *sui generis*. Where Lovecraft excites, Ligotti appals: his world, though dreamlike, is intensely real, and it was fundamental in making me rethink the nature of the relationship between dream reality and waking reality, and drop the many *clichés* I had carried in my lexicon as to how dreams manifested other realities breaking through in mythic form. Now I saw dreams as the unstoppable influx of the other into the totality of our life, not merely small revelations of unearthly beauty with little meaning. Dreams were not only often absolutely real to me, but were now accurate representations of an absolutely trans-dimensional existence. Through them, I think I came as close to understanding Hell as anyone can in purely imagical terms; Tom took me sight-seeing there, and the theological ramifications it had for my ideas have been enormous.

Tom is erudite and unpredictable, as well as one who generously acknowledges those who have fired his work, and his influences on me have been many. He introduced me to the exquisite work—as bleak and beautiful as bone—of Georg Trakl, who remains one of my most-loved writers and one, like Tom, who exists in that crepuscular world between prose and poetry. He made me re-read Cioran, an author whom I enjoyed, though I thought, and still do, that the meaning that arises from the sum of his words doesn't match the ferociously cynical sonority of his language. He suggested the Romanian poet Bacovia to me, though I found that there were limits to the amount of literary misery that I could swallow. Tom gobbled him up, with his endless complaining meditations on funerals, the rain, women lying dead in the streets, their make-up running—I rather found Bacovia reminded me of Max Beerbohm's wonderful parody of a nineteenth century decadent English poet in *Seven Men*'s tale, "Enoch Soames." He is a great admirer, too, of Nabokov, and recommended that writer's autobiographical masterpiece of melancholic reverie, *Speak, Memory*, which shares with Ligotti's prose a sense of dreamlike repetition and evanescent epiphanies, though there is little similarity between Tom's overwhelming bleakness of vision and the cultured and happily jaded *Mittel Europa* ennui that overlays Nabokov's meditations.

Musically, Tom's loves are predictably unpredictable: guitar instrumentals from, predominantly, the 1960s, and surf-guitar music. The Shadows are a particular favourite of his. My Bloody Valentine he spoke highly of, and The Moody Blues. On another plane we met each other, shook hands under some lysergically fallopian moon, and shook heads in front of the speaker bins to Iron Butterfly's fantastic instrumental piece, "Iron Butterfly Theme"; but I still can't follow him to the *Threshold of a Dream* or *Days of Future Past*. Thankfully. Yet—YES: *The Yes Album, Fragile*, and *Tales from Topographic Oceans* still move me as much as Emerson, Lake and Palmer's *Trilogy*. I find it difficult to understand why anyone doesn't love these records. Luckily, I found Tom was one of those who share my admiration for those groups, whose records are now found primarily in bargain bins and the "ironic" section of record collections. But, on balance, Tom would throw his hat into the "more of the instrumental, less of the castrato" corner of the musical world. But I love castrati. They are expensive to keep, but terribly grateful and kind.

Despite Tom's several awards, and praise for his work from such luminaries as Ramsey Campbell and Poppie Z. Brite, he has not gained the wider acceptance he deserves. His vast and diseased world, full of dusty mannequins, soiled wallpaper, prosthetic fakes and vampiric impersonations of the living, is written in a mixture of the colours of cement and peacock. His characters move as shadow-puppets move, badly and lit blurringly, through two-dimensional landscapes cast by dirty lights, tracked under malevolent, spiteful, starlacked skies. The ends to which our schemes and dreams come is of no importance, like our gestures and thoughts: pointless motions of body and mind in a universe of smeared fairground mirrors. This is the Gnostic nightmare *par excellence*. He is the greatest writer of our time in any genre, whether our eyes are closed to his abysmal vision of the overwhelming nature of the sadness and terror of things or not.

EPILOGUE: EXTRACT FROM A LETTER
FROM LIGOTTI TO MYSELF:

TL, 12 January 1997: I never heard of [Tiny Tim's film] *Blood Harvest* but it does sound like something I might find on the horror shelves of the local vid store. Stay stupid, stay alive, those are my words to live by these days. I saw *Mars Attacks*, which absolutely sucked and that's all that deserves to be said about it."

31 VIII 2002

THE DREAM QUEST OF THOMAS LIGOTTI: A STUDY OF *IN A FOREIGN TOWN, IN A FOREIGN LAND*

Ben P. Indick

The genesis of the peculiarly new and individual voice of Thomas Ligotti in horror fiction was as a short story in each of the final four issues of a semi-professional magazine, *Nyctalops,* commencing in March 1981 and concluding in its final issue, a long-delayed and much-regretted decade later in April 1991. The publication had progressed from a mimeographed fanzine to a very professional, if irregularly published, publication printed on good stock and using color in addition to its customary black and white illustrations. It was published by Harry O. Morris, Jr., of Albuquerque, N. Mex., himself a distinguished artist employing photographic collage. It was immediately evident to Morris and his readers (the final number had a 600-copy print run) that Ligotti was unique, and Morris went on to print in 1986 a separate booklet of fiction by him, *Songs of a Dead Dreamer,* a print run of 300 copies which would slowly sell out and finally become a collector's item.[1]

Critical response was slow as well, and Ligotti, whose subsequent books, always collections of short fiction[2], while garnering several awards[3], has always appeared to critics to be "caviare to the general"[4]. As late as 1997, Mike Ashley is quoted in *The Encyclopedia of Fantasy* saying Ligotti "established a cult following for his special brand of horror"[5]. Whether or not his appeal was to cultists alone does not appear to have affected Ligotti, who has continued to write slowly in his own voice, although his styles in different books have varied.

He is quoted on the Internet website pages devoted to him under FAQ (Frequently Asked Questions) as saying that H. P. Lovecraft had the most profound influence on his life rather than his fiction, as reading Lovecraft's work was the impetus for his own writing career. He credits Poe as having the most actual influence on his writing. His self-analysis holds up to the extent that the colorful and ultimately emotional excesses of Poe are reflected in Ligotti; however, the sense of scene, told flatly, however unique (as often gothic as it may be expressionistic) derives from Lovecraft's own superb attention to detail and atmosphere. And Ligotti's atmosphere is unerring. He also credits as influences Vladimir Nabokov, as pointillist a genius as ever penned a jewel-like line, to whom Ligotti's own precision is tribute, and Bruno Schultz, the Polish Jew killed in the Holocaust, whose unnerving and off-kilter *Street of the Crocodiles* made his name famous and left an imprint in the skewed towns and strangely warped reality Ligotti's protagonists wander unknowingly and sometimes aimlessly through.

His earlier stories are, within the narrowly focused parameters of his vision, more traditional, in that there is conversation, social intercourse between individuals, and action leading to reaction. They can be characterized by the "well-known story" he tells in his Introduction to *Noctuary:* "A man awakes in the darkness and reaches over for his eyeglasses on the nightstand. The eyeglasses are placed in his hand."[6] This is,indeed, a genuine and excellent story, but there is both mystery and simultaneously completion, a pat quality at odds with his own particular vision as it would later develop. Again, in his earlier work, Ligotti is more interested in literary tricks and the particular over the general than his later work would demonstrate. Thus, he accomplishes a delightfully different tour de force in *The Agonizing Resurrection of Victor Frankenstein and Other Gothic Tales*[7]. Here he has borrowed the protagonists, heroes and villains (and villainesses) of some twenty real and imaginary characters, from Dr.Frankenstein, the Phantom of the Opera, Poe's William Wilson and the Lady Ligiea, and many others right up to the gaunt figure of H. P. Lovecraft himself, dying in a hospital bed. The collection is filled with humor and insight as well as a soupçon of grue, and even O. Henry type twists at the end of the short stories, hardly characteristic of Ligotti. It remains an off-beat item indicating other directions the author could easily have pursued, but that his intentions lay elsewhere.

The full ripening of Ligotti's style would appear in 1997 in a small edition, both in size and print run, *In A Foreign Town, In A*

Foreign Land [8]. The diminutive book, print run unstated, is only 5" by 7" and 55 pages, is bound in heavy cloth, and decorated with different urban scenes on the front cover, which is neo-expressionistic, and the back cover, which is semi-abstract, but still evidently urban, both by Steven Stapledon. The frontispiece is also by Stapledon, a combined realism with a more contemporary abstract background. Withal, the artwork is an excellent artistic approximation of the characteristically densely textured yet precise prose. The Gothic element, referred to in his *Victor Frankenstein* title(cf 7), is immediately evident over all, in addition to the unquestionable presence of Lovecraft as a mentor in the prose, with relative absence of conversation and the matter of fact descriptions of mundane streets and rooms as well as unnerving incidents and suspicions. Ligotti, however, for the most part avoids Lovecraft's most effective but inevitably melodramatic use of italics, as though high-lighting or underlining horrific climaxes, for there are no horrific climaxes in these Ligotti stories. Italics appear occasionally to highlight specific moments.

Like *Grimscribe* and *Noctuary, In a Foreign Town, In A Foreign Land* is written in the form of a novel, while actually being four short stories, with associations between each. Ligotti is quoted in a 1998 conversation (9) as saying he does not enjoy reading novels, nor would he enjoy writing one. However, despite each being an episode complete initself, the coincidence of certain characters and situations make the totality correspond to a short novel. They are entitled, without intra-title capitalizing, "His shadow shall rise to a higher house," "The bells will sound forever," "A soft voice whispers nothing," and "When you hear the singing, you will know it is time."

The unnamed narrator of "His shadow shall rise to a higher house" speaks from an unnamed town, known only as "a town near the northern border" (p. 1). He tells us of the local hilltop cemetery "that was far more populated than the town over which it hovered" in which is buried the unfortunately repugnant shape of the dead man, Ascrobius. There is a wry quality in Ligotti at times as if the author has his tongue slyly in his cheek, but even if so, his straightforward style of narration never varies. Ascrobius, a sickly, deformed man, has died, nearly anonymously, and been buried, but (and Ligotti deliciously assumes a Lovecraftian italic pose for a moment) there is local talk on "the phenomenon of the grave" (sic)—it is neither empty nor despoiled; it is simply non-existent in the area it was presumed to have been in. Records are not kept in the cemetery of interment sites so certainty is impossible; there remains only, where "there once had been a grave like any other, there was now, in the same precious space, only a patch of virgin earth."

A "Dr. Klatt" appears, insisting he knew the deceased and had been treating him. He even insists on seeing the name of ASCROBIUS on the headstone, although it is apparently empty of words, a not uncommon situation in the ancient cemetery. He often calls him a "monster" or a "freak." His patient, he says, had had "incredible powers . . . might even have cured himself of his diseased physical condition," but what he had sought, Klatt insists, was not a cure but total annulment of his self, uncreation of his entire life (p. vi). Hysterical individuals have never been rare in this town, but after the disappearance of the grave, they have increased. Reverberant screams are heard in the town at dead of night (p. vii). Klatt enlists the aid of an innkeeper, Mrs. Glimm, who will reappear in other stories, whose inn is probably a brothel for travelers, and sends an uneducated but attractive woman to investigate the presumed tombsite in the dark of night. She does not return, which seems to bother no one, for talk of Ascrobius remains their topic. (p. ix). When investigation commences, her dismembered body, arranged roughly in the shape of the tomb, is there. On Klatt's advice they leave it there. Klatt departs. The house of the uncreated Ascrobius occasionally has uncommon lights or noises and people worry that one day perhaps other homes may be uncreated. "Nor do I welcome the thought that one day someone may notice that a particular house appears to be missing, or absent, from the place it once occupied along the backstreet of a town near the northern border." (p. xi)

Before continuing with the stories, it must be mentioned that the book is accompanied by a CD created by David Tibet, and played by his musical group Current 93. The group has dozens of other releases, but Tibet wrote in a 1996 interview included in the Ligotti Internet website that he considered Ligotti "one of the greatest authors who has worked in the entire field of visionary and apocalyptic literature." He interpreted these stories musically together with Steven Stapleton and Christoph Heeman. Ligotti as well as severaloloists contributed. It has four continuous and unbroken bands, each approximately fifteen minutes, and successively named for each story. The sound track, which the reader is urged by a liner note to "listen to at low volume, at dusk, while reading (the book)" is a remarkably symbiotic companion to the words, some of which are occasionally heard over a continuous and moody background, in which pronounced melody is scarce, and atmosphere is all. Initially the unlocking and opening of a door is heard, followed by a throbbing sound, while a voice, possibly that of the author, reads some of the text, with a lyrical, poetic quality, so that the listener, book in hand, is nearly able to envision Ligotti's characters and situations. It ceases abruptly as night sounds emerge. In the mélange of sound, it is nearly impossible to distinguish any particular instrument, although the liner credits the several players with their particular instrument. There are occasional whistling sounds; the wind howls; nothing is prelude, all is composition and all defers to the essence, the sense of the book.

The narrator of the second story, "The bells will sound forever" is sitting in a park when a gentleman, a commercial traveler, "who looked as if he should be in a hospital" (p. xii) sits nearby. His appearance is left unexplored, but the man tells of visits as a commercial representative to a northern town, to an inn, not Mrs. Glimm's brothel-inn. The landlady of this inn, Mrs. Pyk, has her own special properties. She is alleged to have been a sideshow dancer and later a fortune-teller, and her inn is located in a dark, unused part of town. She has an artificial hand, although the other is palsied and as ugly, and there are no other guests. He fears he has made a bad miscalculation coming here, but signs the register, "Q. H. Crumm."

He is not comforted when she deposits him on the highest floor, and as they walk up, he hears, although indistinctly, the jangling of bells outside; he is surprised to feel not tired but peculiarly titillated and excited. Only the attic is above him, and, anxious to see it, he goes up. It is a cramped room, although the house itself is spacious. It is filled with costumes and posters of days when Mrs.

Pyk was an exotic dancer and later a fortune teller. It is a "paradise of the past" (p. xx). He discovers a fool's costume, hat and traditional accoutrements (p. xx) and dresses in it. It is lined with little bells. He hears the bells again, and falls to the floor, where he sleeps. He hears the bells, awakes and sees Mrs Pyk. "Open your eyes . . . and see your surprise,"(p. xxi) a voice says, and when he does, he sees himself as a jester's head on a wooden stick in her wooden hand. He fades out of consciousness. When he awakes, he is on his bed, clothed and Mrs. Pyk is shaking him, telling him he must go to work. He leaves reluctantly, wanting to return, but when he does, he discovers her house has burned down. Perhaps she had feuded, some people mutter, with Mrs. Glimm, her competitor, and he hears rumors that people who stayed too long at Mrs. Pyk's never left. Bodies are actually found in the remains of the hotel, but never hers. He always hears the bells now. He concludes his story and simply stares ahead of him. The narrator thinks about him, about Mrs. Pyk and especially of the bells, which he almost imagines he can hear. He fears someone else's dream has preoccupied him. "Perhaps this dream ultimately belongs to no one, however many persons, including commercial agents, may have belonged to it," are the concluding words of this superb story.

Current 93 and David Tibet interpret this story atmospherically with a nearly ceaseless sound, now loud, now nearly inaudible, of a wind chime-like sound, accompanied at times by throbbing. Early on, a man's voice appears to ask for a room. Later, a woman's voice, more clearly and obviously Mrs. Pyk, tells him to "open your eyes . . . and see your surprise" which of course, he does, reading clearly with horror of seeing his head as a jester, "a single consuming thought," italicized by Ligotti, *to be a head on a stick held in the wooden hand of Mrs. Pyk. Forever . . . forever."* The sound abruptly ceases an instant later and Mrs. Pyk's voice is clearly heard telling him: "Wake up, Mr. Crumm. It's late and you have to be on your way. You have business across the border." Tibet and Ligotti have chosen not to opt for the melodramatic, for this band might well have used traditional music to allude to Mrs. Pyk's circus background, nor have they attempted to capture the burning of her hotel and her disappearance. Like the author himself, it underplays its own lines.

In the third, and shortest, story, "A soft voice whispers nothing," the narrator tells us that long before he had actually known of the existence of the town near the northern border, he believed he was already an inhabitant there. He had been sickly during childhood, which might be a reference to Lovecraft's childhood. He remembers how the "dull winter days were succeeded by blinding winter nights" (p. xxviii). His physician, Dr. Zirk, appears to have a physical affinity for the cold northern border town, and espouses a state of not existing. Later he finds the northern town bare, vacant-looking, as though a great photographic flash had frozen the scene. It is an hallucinogenic scene, Bosch-like, as he watches an eerie procession in the streets, a figure with "an egg-shaped head that was completely hairless and as white as paste, a clown of some kind" (p. xxxi) followed by others, a "team of ragged men who were harnessed like beasts and pulled long bristling ropes" (p. xxxi) attached to a wooden-wheeled wagon whose surface had bars erected from which hung an assembly of ill-assorted articles, "masks and shoes, household utensils and naked dolls, large bleached bones and the skeletons of small animals . . . all knocking together in a wild percussion." He is accosted by Mrs. Glimm, whose fat fingers wear many gaudy rings. She encourages him to stay at her lodging-house and gives him a paper bearing a "metaphysical lecture," (p. xxxiv) which he studies, and he hears a voice intoning more of it as he sleeps. He thinks of Dr Zirk who had long ago described his home as an "architectural moan" (p. xxxv). The voice continues. "All our ecstasies, whether sacred or from the slime, depend on our refusal to be schooled in even the most superficial truths and our maddening will to follow the path of forgetfulness. Amnesia may well be the highest sacrament in the great gray ritual of existence." (p. xxxvii) The next morning he awakens to "the same delicious cacophony I had heard the day before" (p.xxxviii), but there is no corresponding parade. He only sees a window from which the body of a man is hanging by a rope. The body is that of Dr. Zirk. And now the parade re-commences, beneath Dr. Zirk's body, and a hand, whose heavy fingers bear many rings, appears, holding a razor. The hand slashes the rope and Dr. Zirk's body falls into the familiar wagon. The narrator is motionless, staring endlessly out the window "upon the town that I knew was my home." (p.xl)

For this story, with its highly visible elements, Tibet allows more expression of its elements. Barking sounds, noise, murmurs of music and singing, whistles and steam emanations, perhaps the groans of the rolling wooden-wheeled wagon, and finally a near-languorous melody, fading away. Interestingly, Stapleton's art for the CD record itself, while very similar to the illustration on the cover of the book, has an extra feature: an empty hangman's noose hangs from a building's roof.

In the final, fourth tale, "When you hear the singing, you will know it is time," the narrator may, or may not, be the narrator of the previous story, but he has "lived in the town near the northern border long enough so that, without fully knowing it, I had begun to believe that I would never leave there, at least not while I was alive." (p. xli) One night he wakes up, hearing words being intoned from the basement of his rooming house. He discovers beneath the worn carpet, a trapdoor, covered with a sort of worn and cracked leather. He touches it and feels it vibrating to the intoning voice below, but does not lift it. The following day he wanders the town, and here Ligotti revels in the gothic wonders of classic expression-ist art, examining how "the buildings seem to have grown into one another, melding their diverse materials into a bizarre and jagged conglomerate of massive architectural proportions, its peaked roofs and soaring chimnied towers visibly swaying and audibly moaning." (p. cxlv). This was not all, however, for passersby would speak an "incantation to whomever would listen. 'When you hear the singing,' they said, 'you will know it is time.'"(p. xlvi).

At the same time, the population of the town appears to be thinning out. "Disappearances," (p. xlvii) some say, in vague de-scription. (10) One of them is the "demonic preacher, Rev. Cork" (p. lii). Some think he is the leader of an invisible demon town; possi-bly the intonations the narrator had heard were the Reverend be-neath his trapdoor. Townspeople sneer at the narrator and say if he had looked beneath it he would not be here now. Perhaps "it was only a matter of time before your world, whatever you thought it to be, was undermined, if not completely overrun, by another world." (p. liii) Finally he leaves his room, wanders to the cemetery atop the hill, stays all night in the dampness and realizes now he will not die in this northern border town, will not be buried here, and has wandered the streets for the last time. He knows intuitively and disquietingly that the thoughts he has had of demon towns are "chaos and insanity" (p. liv). Indeed the story may be taken as a study of paranoia infecting an individual and a town. He leaves. Years later he learns that government investigators had come to the town and found it nearly deserted, the only inhabitants left being mad old men and women who walked about muttering of "other towns" or "demon towns." Among them is an old woman, heavy and dressed gaudily, the owner of a lodging house and other property, now useless, she says, for any practical purposes. The investigators agree, finding that whatever else the town appeared to be it was "always a genius of the most insidious illusions." (p. lv)

The beautiful title is the substance of the final band of the record. It is initially repeated over and over again, beyond even its appearances in the story. However, it is all important to the narrator, for it is comprehensible in personal terms to him. It eventually fades away, as does the long and eloquent musical coda, fading into inaudibility at last, without any false climactic chord at all.

There is a similarity between the climax of the story and the opening of "The Shadow Over Innsmouth," the Lovecraft classic story of a town whose essential nature has been corrupted by an alien species. Ligotti's own genius has made the story wholly his own, whether or not debts to prior writers exist.

Liogotti remains active, and has announced another collaboration with Current 93, using "12 short texts" by him, and entitled "I Have a Special Plan for This World." Quite unexpectedly, for a reader accustomed to his stories so spare in conversation, he has also been working on screenplays, and collaborated with Brandon Tranz, a co-worker at Gale Research, where Ligotti was an editor for two decades, in 1998 on one for the television show, *The X-Files* (as yet unproduced but scheduled for publication by David Tibet's Durtro in 2002) and has work optioned by the films. The dialogue should at the least be unusual, but if the work is pure Ligotti, the atmosphere should be haunting. Surprisingly, he is quoted by Carl

T. Ford as saying he "never found writing stories much fun" but enjoyed the collaboration on the screenplay.

Whatever his path, the brilliance of *In A Foreign Town, In A Foreign Land* remains a high point of his career and the most individual accomplishment of his art. It establishes him as a writer beyond being the idol of cults. Given his increasingly widespread interests, and even a possible desire to avoid being pigeonholed into one particular mode, this remarkable book may remain a literary oddity in Ligotti's *oeuvre*. Having previously demonstrated success within the usual parameters of story-telling, i.e., characters, situation and denouement, *In A Foreign Town, In A Foreign Land* represents the exploration and summation of a lone aspect of his creative mind, the subconscious, touched upon but never as comprehensively in some prior stories, in a microscopic examination of a scene which while broadly abstract is in its particulars concrete, thus remaining only vaguely realized. Confined as it is to a single site, within a very consistent mood, and employing a cast of clearly delineated, if decidedly unusual, character-types, it holds the mystery and beauty as well as the unsettling quality of a subtly told prose poem or a musical composition. It is hardly surprising that the thematic musicalization has proven equally consistent. Yet, to seek to replicate the story's success would possibly invite only repetition. Ligotti is too patient a writer and thinker to attempt such useless gratification. He has successfully completed his dream-quest here, and it may remain a solitary one.

NOTES:

1. *Songs of a Dead Dreamer* was revised and printed, less several and with several new stories added, in the hardcover edition of the same title published in 1990 by Carroll and Graf Publishers, Inc., New York.

2. *Grimscribe* (Carroll and Graf Publishers, New York, 1991) is presented in novel form, without a contents page other than subdivision into five groupings of short stories, all more or less associated with the observer Grimscribe, "His Lives and Works," and the four stories which comprise *In A Foreign Town, In A Foreign Land* (Durtro, 1997) have some common elements.

3. *The Nightmare Factory* (Carroll and Graf Publishers, New York 1996) a collection of short stories, some reprinted from previ-

ous collections, received the prestigious Stoker awards from the Horror Writers Association for Best Author, Best Collection and also for Best Novella for the story, "The Red Tower."

4. "caviare to the general." *Hamlet,* Act II, Scene 2

5. *The Encyclopedia of Fantasy,* edited by John Clute and John Grant (St. Martins Press, New York, 1997) pg.581.

6. *Noctuary* (Carroll andGraf Publishers, New York, 1994) Foreword, p. viii.

7. *The Agonizing Resurrection of Victor Frankenstein and Other Gothic Tales,* (Silver Salamander Press, 1994).

8. *In A Foreign Town, In A Foreign Land,* Durtro, 1997.

9. *Dagon,* Sept.-Dec. 1998,"Notes on the Writing of Horror. An Interview with Thomas Ligotti," by Carl T.Ford.

10. Interestingly, Ligotti is quoted in another interview with Carl B. Ford, on "Terror Tales Online Website" as saying, relevant to these disappearances, "I think Lovecraft would also have made fine fictional use of the rash of suicide cults in recent decades."

LIGOTTI'S CORPORATE HORROR

Darrell Schweitzer

"Searchers after horror," wrote Lovecraft, "haunt strange, far places. For them are the catacombs of Ptolemais, and the carven mausolea of the nightmare countries." So begins "The Picture in the House," which then demonstrates that horror is likewise to be found a lot closer to home, in Lovecraft's case, in the Massachusetts countryside.

Thomas Ligotti surely agrees. He and his readers need look no further than the nearest office highrise to find the true stuff of dread and terror.

As of this writing, Ligotti's most recently published fictions all fall into the category of "corporate horror," i.e. the horror of the workplace, of the dehumanizing effects of large, cubicle-filled offices where vast numbers of anonymous, white-collar drones waste their lives on meaningless tasks. Think of the comic-strip *Dilbert* in prose, as a collaboration between Franz Kafka and Edgar Allan Poe at his most maniacal, and you get something of the idea.

Two stories in what may yet turn into a series, about the luckless wage-slaves of the "Quine Organization," have appeared in *Weird Tales,* and are as yet uncollected. They are one step beyond *In a Foreign Town, In a Foreign Land*, taking place in unnamed, fog-filled factory towns "beyond the border."

Beyond the border of what, we may reasonably ask. At one point a narrator comments that the commercial organization and the political entity, the nation, have "approached total assimilation of one by the other."

In the first story, "My Case for Retributive Action," the nameless narrator assumes his new job as a "processor of forms" at "a storefront office" in a typically depressing, grungy, Ligotti-esque town. The work is, of course, meaningless in the extreme. We never find out what exactly the Quine Organization produces or sells. There are merely endless piles of paperwork. The town itself seems to be controlled by the Organization, which runs the apartment houses, pharmacies, medical establishments, etc. and keeps its employees docile with the drugs they need to survive the futile grind of the Quine experience. (Indeed the narrator apparently got this job on the recommendation of his doctor, as a part of his therapy.)

In the course of things, a fellow employee, whom our anxiety-ridden narrator finds "unendurable," takes the narrator to lunch (but no lunch is served) and tells the story of a second employee, who snapped under the strain, created a scene at the office, was fired and soon after found dead. A third employee, who may be a company spy, takes the narrator aside and explains that everything the first fellow said is a lie.

Meanwhile, there are odd rumors of a "spider thing" seen creeping about the town, a "nobby monster" with "a protrusion from his body that looked very much like a human head." The employee who went mad, by the way, had a terrible spider-phobia. By the time the story is over, we find he had more than that. In the narrator's dusty, vermin-filled room is discovered the "spider thing" itself, which is the missing man, degenerated into a nightmarish monstrosity for want of the essential drugs that kept him human in a Quine-dominated environment. The hero kills this thing to put it out of its misery, but he also extracts two vials of its venom, with which he is to carry out his revenge, first against his doctor-therapist, then against (presumably) the company. The narrator addresses his entire narrative and offers the second vial to another (equally disturbed) person, who will presumably do harm with it.

In the semi-sequel, "Our Temporary Supervisor," an anonymous narrator (possibly the same person, though there is no indication of it) puts aside any youthful dreams he might have had of a more interesting life and accepts a dead-end job at a Quine Organization factory. Instead of shuffling papers, he works non-stop, with barely time off for sleep, assembling incomprehensible metal parts. The job is easy, the fellow workers "congenial enough," though a more mind-numbing existence would be hard to imagine. Again, we are in a gloomy, fog-filled company town near the "border." Again, the company provides the essential anxiety-drugs which make life minimally bearable.

One day the regular supervisor goes away on "company business," and is replaced by . . . something. Again a single employee snaps, storms into the office and meets an unknowable fate. The narrator, remembering vaguely that he once aspired to more in life, tries to resign, only to be told by the company's telephone operator that "the company is not accepting resignations at this time." He is trapped in the gray purgatory of the workplace, dependent on the company for drugs, until eventually he becomes (presumably) a model employee and stops thinking about anything at all.

Ligotti's most elaborate fictional response to the workplace is found in his recent book, *My Work Is Not Yet Done: Three Tales of Corporate Horror*. The feature item here, the title story, runs 142 pages. It is a novella, the longest piece Ligotti has yet written. Given his frequently-repeated statements about novels—that he does not particularly like them and cannot imagine himself writing one—this seems to be the closest thing we may ever see to an actual Ligotti novel.

The narrator, again, is a typical, suffering, anxiety-ridden Ligotti drone, as sensitive as Roderick Usher, as obsessive as any number of other Poe (or Lovecraft) characters, a youngish man given to nursing every hurt and humiliation, whether real or otherwise, ranging from the trivial (the theft of a roll of postage stamps from his cubicle) to more serious (the callous disregard, then theft of a major new product idea, on which our hero has worked long and hard). He has been, he informs us, afraid all his life. Life itself is a meaningless horror. The "grand scheme of things," the meaning of existence is simply this:

A: There is no grand scheme of things.
B: If there were a grand scheme of things, the fact—the *fact*—that we are not equipped to perceive it, either by natural or supernatural means, is a nightmarish obscenity.
C: The very notion of a grand scheme of things is a nightmarish obscenity. (p. 23)

The protagonist (who actually has a name this time, though his boss keeps getting it wrong) seems to be going off the deep end in a manner all too familiar in corporate America. He plans revenge. He buys guns and knives. He empties out his bank account, a sure sign in the modern world that one does not propose to go on living. But, before he can release a manifesto of his grievances or return to his workplace and slaughter everyone . . . something happens. He is not sure what. He finds himself transformed into a superman, with amazing powers, who is able to eliminate the hated inner circle of the office one by one, in increasingly imaginative and impossible ways. One victim vanishes into the woodwork. Another is found amid a grotesque "museum" of dolls and manikins, turned into a dummy herself, complete with internal organs made of plaster. Another physically absorbed by the hideous "human garbage can" in a sado-masochistic, bondage club. This goes on until the protagonist finally confronts his nemesis, the boss, only to come to some understanding: that he was hit by a truck and is lying in a coma. His career of vengeance has been accomplished out-of-body, though the results are apparently quite real, not illusions or dreams. But he can only kill so many, and now he has one choice left, before he runs out of energy. He can wipe out the boss, *or* he can go back to the hospital ward where his physical self lies, and kill himself—this being his one and only chance to escape the horror of existence. He takes this latter course.

The volume also contains a short story, "I Have A Special Plan for This World," set in an office where the emotional tension is like a (literal) fog, so thick that the narrator can hardly see three feet in front of himself. When he finally confronts the disembodied "presence" of the corporation in a lavatory, he breaks a window to allow the "presence" to pour into the city outside. The crime rate goes up. The city becomes known as Murder Town.

The book closes with "The Nightmare Network," a series of bizarre and surreal "advertisements" and memos which could only come from the world of Ligotti Incorporated.[1]

What does all of this mean? At one level, it is clear that these are some of the most autobiographical of Thomas Ligotti's fictions. Of course it is dangerous to attempt biographical criticism on a living author, particularly one who has been as reclusive as Ligotti. No one in our field has met him, though he is a friendly correspondent and has submitted to a number of interviews, either by mail or over the internet.

From published statements in interviews, some of which are included in the present volume, a general picture emerges. Ligotti has not had a particularly happy life, and, after some youthful experiments with drugs (and possibly before) has suffered from severe anxiety disorders. These are impossible for someone who has not experienced them to fully comprehend, but the key to the problem is a "panic attack," which is like a fire-alarm going off in the brain, leading to blind, unreasoning panic. Such a reaction has survival value if, say, one is swimming and about to be swallowed by a great white shark, but for an anxiety-disorder sufferer, there are "false alarms" which are themselves so terrifying that the victim rearranges his whole life to avoid their recurrence. If this develops into agoraphobia, literally the "fear of the marketplace"—surely a loaded phrase in Corporate America—the agoraphobe may become unable to travel more than a few minutes from home, and only to familiar places, or he may even become housebound. The reaction of such a person when pushed to their (very narrow) limits—which might be as trivial as crossing a parking lot—reportedly resembles the kind of unease the rest of us might feel if tottering at a cliff's edge a thousand feet up. There is no real cure, though some people achieve symptom-relief by drugging themselves into a semi-stupor, which is surely not a viable option for a sensitive, artistic sort. Most phobics stop fighting their condition as they get older, and live increasingly restrictive lives.

The narrator of "My Case for Retributive Action," addressing the mysterious other, utters what is surely a cry from the heart:

> I know that your condition differs from mine, and therefore you have no means by which to fully comprehend my ordeals, just as I cannot fully comprehend yours. But I do acknowledge that both our conditions are unendurable, despite the doctor's second-hand platitude that nothing in this world is unendurable. I have come to believe that the world itself, by its very nature, is unendurable. It is only our responses to this fact that deviate: mine being predominantly a response of passive terror approaching absolute panic; yours being predominantly a response of gruesome obsessions that you fear you might act upon. (pp. 32-33)

We consider further the last ravings of the protagonist of "My Work Is Not Yet Done":

> ... my Ultimate Statement, as I now attempt to deliver it to you, not one of whom will ever benefit from it. People do not know, and cannot face, the things that go on in this world, the secret nightmares that are suffered by millions every day ... and the excruciating paradox, the nightmarish obscenity of being something that does not know what it is and yet believes it does know, something that in fact is nothing but a tiny particle that forms the body of The Great Black Swine Which Wallows in a Great River of Blackness that looks to us like sunrises and skyscrapers, like all the knotted events of the past and the unraveling of these knots in the future, like birthdays and funerals, like satellites and cell phones and rockets launched into space, like nations and peoples, like the laws of nature and the laws of humanity, like families and friends, like everything, including these words that I write. (p. 153)

There is considerable irony in all this. The character in "My Case for Retributive Action" inflicts a hideous doom upon his therapist, all the while reassuring him, as he himself had been reassured, that "nothing is unendurable." The narrator of "My Work Is Not Yet Done" is over-the-top more often than not, as grim and as funny similtaneously as Montressor in Poe's "A Cask of Amontillado." There is always an arch detachment in Ligotti's fiction. His stories are not painful, self-pitying cries; they are *appreciations* of the absurdity of existence. Small surprise that the god of the small town of Mirocaw is a harlequin.[2] This attitude is consistent throughout the whole body of Ligotti's work, whose dominant characteristic may be therefore described, not as *horror* or *fear*, but truly dark and terrible laughter. His fiction is decidedly post-modern in that it is completely self-aware. His narrators, (such as the one in "My Work Is Not Yet Done," quoted above, or, even more memorably, that of the masterful "Nethescurial"), often subtly mocking us, extrapolate the absurdity and unreliability of the universe into their own words, into the text itself.

This being so, an autobiographical reading of Ligotti's corporate stories seems to work, but is itself an imaginative construct of limited usefulness. True, Mr. Ligotti recently quit a long-held office job and removed himself from Michigan to Florida, an uprooting which cannot have been easy for someone who suffers from anxiety disorders. True, too, he used to live in Detroit, which is known as the murder capital of the USA, whether this was caused by a golden miasma pouring out of the broken window of a corporate restroom or not. Only Ligotti knows how much is really "true," and he may find the definition of truth fluid, or even moot.

It is safer to say, then, that these stories read as if written with great conviction—at the same time they persist in reminding us of their artificiality through their various, elaborate narrative devices. They are perhaps as autobiographical the stories of Franz Kafka—another keen appreciator of the bleak absurdity of existence. Kafka was never literally transformed into an enormous "vermin" (an insect, not specifically a cockroach), but he wrote as if he had been, as if he knew what it felt like.

Certainly the Quine Organization manages to push every phobic button, to inflict on its victims every possible anxiety-heightening experience. These "corporate horror" stories certainly read as if they are personal nightmares, born out of experience.

It is a safe bet that, at the end at least, Thomas Ligotti didn't like his job and did not flourish in an office environment. It is less certain that he ever turned into a supernatural, out-of-body, mass-murderer or degenerated into a "spider thing." It may well be that he has learned to cope with the awfulness of reality through the metafictional constructs of his fiction—by recognizing the joke of human existence and learning to laugh at it.

NOTES:

1. For example:

Memo from the CEO

As the forces operating in today's marketplace become more shadowy and incomprehensible we must commit ourselves every second of every day to a ceaseless striving for that elusive dream which we all share and which none of us can remember, if it ever existed in the first place. And if anyone thinks that, as all the world races toward the same elusive dream, our competition isn't fully prepared to gnaw off its own genitals to get to the promised land before us and keep it for themselves . . . think again.

2. In "The Last Feast of Harlequin."

WORKS CITED:

Ligotti, Thomas. "My Case for Retributive Action." *Weird Tales,* Vol 57, No. 4, #324, Summer 2001.

_____. "Our Temporary Supervisor." *Weird Tales,* Vol 58, No. 1, #325, Fall 2001.

_____. *My Work Is Not Yet Done: Three Tales of Corporate Horror.* Poplar Bluff, MO: Mythos Books, 2002.

THOMAS LIGOTTI:
THE ESCAPE FROM LIFE

S. T. Joshi

"There is no field other than the weird in which I have any aptitude or inclination for fictional composition. Life has never interested me so much as the escape from life" (Lovecraft [1971], p. 395). Ironically, this utterance by H. P. Lovecraft was made when he was well into what he himself called his "quasi-realistic" (Lovecraft [1976], p. 170) phase, in which the weird is introduced subtly and gradually through the painstaking accumulation of realistic details in every aspect of the tale except that pertaining to the weird manifestation. And that Lovecraft was far from truly wishing for an "escape from life" is evident in his earnest concern for economic justice and political reform as the depression of the 1930s ground on. *At the Mountains of Madness* could only have been written by one for whom the real world manifestly exists.

The whole notion of escaping from life—escaping, that is, from the mundane, the actual, the real—can apply much more pertinently to a recent writer, Thomas Ligotti. Ligotti's interest is focused more intensely on the weird, and only on the weird, than any author in the history of weird fiction. I do not think it would be possible to study, for example, the sociopolitical aspects of Ligotti's fiction—there do not seem to be any. His portrayal of human relationships, when it occurs at all, is either perfunctory or sardonic. Human characters, indeed, are virtually insignificant in themselves in his work, serving only as embodiments of or conduits to the unreal.

Ligotti is himself one of the strangest phenomena in weird fiction, not only for the utter bizarrerie of his own work but for the curious way in which he has emerged as a leading writer in the field. Having published a certain number of stories in fan magazines (*Nyctalops*) or what might at best be called "semi-pro" magazines (*Fantasy Tales, Eldritch Tales*) in the early 1980s, Ligotti issued a collection of short stories, *Songs of a Dead Dreamer,* from the specialty firm of Silver Scarab Press, operated by Harry O. Morris, Jr.

When this volume emerged in 1986, Ligotti was still almost entirely unknown: I myself received a review copy of it and rather hastily and ignorantly dismissed it as mere "fan fiction." But Morris had, as it were, backed the right horse, for very shortly thereafter Ligotti was embraced by many of the leading writers and critics of the field (Ramsey Campbell had written an introduction to *Songs of a Dead Dreamer*) and his reputation began to grow, although still in a sort of subterranean fashion. A British trade paperback of his collection, augmented with new stories (and, it must be admitted, with some of the more embarrassingly poor ones removed), emerged in 1989; this was reprinted in hardcover in this country in 1990 and in paperback the next year. A second and still more substantial collection, *Grimscribe,* appeared in late 1991, and a third collection, *Noctuary,* was published in 1994. Liggoti is, however, still content to publish the majority of his work in the small press, although he has made occasional forays into full-fledged professional journals (*The Magazine of Fantasy & Science Fiction*) and anthologies (Douglas E. Winter's *Prime Evil,* 1988). Perhaps this is just as well, for his work is certainly not best-seller material in the manner of Stephen King's or Clive Barker's.

If Ligotti's refreshing lack of self-promotion is virtually unique in what has become the big-business world of weird fiction, then his actual work is also entirely original and unclassifiable. His is the most distinctive voice in the field. This is not to say that he is necessarily the best weird fictionist now writing—Ramsey Campbell and T. E. D. Klein, at least, are still his superiors—but his work is perhaps the most easily recognizable of any current writer's because of its sheer difference from that of his contemporaries. Ligotti is one of the few modern weird writers to draw extensively from the older masters of the weird tale—Poe, Lovecraft, Blackwood, Machen—but his work is so far from being pastiche that it is difficult in all but a few cases to pinpoint actual literary influences.

The focus of all Ligotti's work is a systematic assault on the real world and the replacement of it with the unreal, the dream-like, and the hallucinatory. Reality is, for Ligotti, a "grossly overrated affair" ("Alice's Last Adventure" [SDD, p. 38-39]). It is simply too prosy and dull, lacking in intrinsic value or dramatic interest: "It would be difficult to conceive of a creature for whom this world—its bare form seen with open eyes—represented a coveted paradise" ("Vastarien" [SDD, p. 263]). Accordingly, Ligotti's literary goal is to suggest that other realm which we glimpse either through dreams or, worse, stumble upon by accident in obscure corners of this world. Ligotti has neatly summed up his aesthetic of the weird in "The Consolations of Horror," a magnificent essay that ranks among his finest works:

> The horror story does the work of a certain kind of dream we all know. Sometimes it does this so well that even the most irrational and unlikely subject matter can infect the reader with a sense of realism beyond the realistic, a trick usually not seen outside the vaudeville of sleep. When is the last time you failed to be fooled by a nightmare, didn't suspend disbelief because its incidents weren't sufficiently true-to-life? The horror story is only true to dreams, especially those which involve us in mysterious ordeals, the passing of secrets, the passages of forbidden knowledge, and, in more ways than one, the spilling of guts. ("Consolations," p. 48)

This tells us many things: the importance and prevalence of dream-imagery in Ligotti's work; the scorn of the "true-to-life"; and the notion of the quest—the quest for "secrets" and "knowledge" of the realm of the unreal. I shall examine all these points more detailedly later, but what I wish to consider now is the difficulty of classifying Ligotti's work within the standard distinctions existing within the weird tale. Many of his tales do not conform to the conventions of supernatural horror, which Maurice Lévy has compactly defined as work in which "the irrational makes an irruption into the real world" (Lévy, p. 107): the "real world" exists so fragmentarily for Ligotti that the contrast between the "natural" and the "supernatural" is never sufficiently established. This is not (or not yet) meant as a criticism, but simply as a defining characteristic of Ligotti's writing. Nor can his tales be classified as "fantasy" (by which I mean the otherworldly fantasy of a Dunsany or Tolkien) because they are set in what is more or less recognizable as the "real world," but a real world depicted so sketchily—and, perhaps, with such a lack of enthusiasm—that its sole function seems to be as a springboard for the beyond. "Victor Keirion belonged to that wretched sect of souls who believe that the only value of this world lies in its power—at certain times—to suggest another world" ("Vastarien" [SDD, p. 263]). Ligotti in fact rejects such divisions in weird fiction as ontological or psychological horror:

> What seems important to me is not whether the spectre is within or outside of a character . . . but the power of the language and images of a story and the ultimate vision that they help to convey. For all that, everything that happens in every story ever written is merely an event in someone's imagination—exactly as are dreams, which take place on their own little plane of unreality, a realm of nowhere in which outside and inside are of equivalent ontological status, where within is without and both are phantasmal in essence. (F, p. 33)

And yet, does Ligotti flee from the real world simply because it is boring or "overrated"? In "Professor Nobody's Little Lectures on Supernatural Horror" he speaks of the "logic of supernatural horror" as "a logic that is founded on fear; it is a logic whose sole principle states: 'Existence equals Nightmare.' Unless life is a dream, nothing makes sense. For as a reality, it is a rank failure" (SDD, p. 206). Compare this with the character in "The Mystics of Muelenberg" who has found "a greater truth: that all is unreal" (G, p.112-13), or of the narrator of "Allan and Adelaide: An Arabesque": "I have seen the soul of the universe . . . and it is insane" (p. 13), or of the narrator of "The Sect of the Idiot": "Life is the nightmare that leaves its mark upon you in order to prove that it is, in fact, real" (SDD, p. 234), or of a random remark in "In the Shadow of Another World" that speaks of the "marriage of insanity and metaphysics" (G, p. 130). What statements like this suggest is that what we all take to be the real world is actually unreal and also mad. Consider "The Journal of J. P. Drapeau":

> From the earliest days of man there has endured the conviction that there is an order of existence which is entirely strange to him. It does indeed seem that the strict order of the visible world is only a semblance, one providing certain gross materials

which become the basis for subtle improvisations of invisible powers. Hence, it may appear to some that a leafless tree is not a tree but a signpost to another realm; that an old house is not a house but a thing possessing a will of its own; that the dead may throw off that heavy blanket of earth to walk in their sleep, and in ours. And these are merely a few of the infinite variations on the themes of the natural order as it is usually conceived.

But is there really a strange world? Of course. Are there, then, two worlds? Not at all. There is only our own world and it alone is alien to us, intrinsically so by virtue of its lack of mysteries. (SDD, p. 257)

This utterance conveys perhaps as succinctly as any Ligotti's own quest: it is not, in the end, a replacement of the real world by the unreal, but a sort of turning the real world inside out to show that it was unreal all along.

The vehicle for this transformation is language. Ligotti has evolved a highly distinctive and idiosyncratic style that, with seeming effortlessness, metamorphoses existence into nightmare. It closest analogy, on purely stylistic grounds, is the eccentric idiom of M. P. Shiel, although he is not a writer whom Ligotti acknowledges as an influence or model. And yet, the analogy is apt in more than one way. Lovecraft referred to Shiel's "Xélucha" as a "noxiously hideous fragment" (Lovecraft [2000], p. 56), and much of Ligotti's work could be so labeled: it stylistically echoes Shiel's tortuous, metaphor-laden prose-poetry while at the same time seeking to capture that atmosphere of nightmarish or hallucinatory strangeness that typifies Shiel's best short work. Plot is almost everywhere negligible, and everything is subordinate to mood. There is also in Ligotti also a considerable dose of Blackwood's searching exploration of the precise psychological effect of the weird upon human consciousness.

Ligotti, indeed, in essays, interviews, and stories, talks much of style and language, and every one of his stories, successful or otherwise, is written with impeccable meticulousness. In speaking of the need for subtlety in relating a weird tale, Ligotti has remarked that "extraordinary subjects require a certain deviousness in the telling, that a twisted or obscure technique is needed to realize the maximum power of the strange" (R, p. 21). This is reminiscent of T. S. Eliot's celebrated justification for the obscurity of Modernist poetry: "We can only say that it appears likely that poets in our civilization, as it exists at present, must be *difficult*. Our civilization comprehends great variety and complexity, and this variety and complexity, playing upon a refined sensibility, must produce various and complex results. The poet must become more and more comprehensive, more allusive, more indirect, in order to force, to dislocate if necessary, language into his meaning" (Eliot, p. 248). The resemblance may in fact not be entirely adventitious: the absence of any vivid or realistic description of the contemporary world gives Ligotti's tales a curiously archaic cast, but in their allusiveness and disregard for the mechanics of plot they are strikingly modern. However much Ligotti draws upon the weird masters of the early part of the century, his work could only have been written by one sensitive to the ambiguities of this *fin de siècle*. If he errs rather more frequently than I would like on the side of excessive obscurity and excessive plotlessness, and if his style remains just on this side (and sometimes on the other side) of bombast and fustian, then it is perhaps an occupational hazard in the sort of highly intellectualized and self-conscious weird fiction Ligotti has chosen to write.

One of Ligotti's many distinctive attributes is the frequency with which he can metafictionally enunciate his own literary agenda in his tales. Many of his stories are just as much about the writing of horror tales as they are horror tales. In "The Frolic," a psychiatrist's report of a madman's visions are uncannily like Ligotti's own aesthetic quest for the unreal:

> "There's actually quite a poetic geography to his interior dreamland as he describes it. He talked about a place that sounded like the back alleys of some cosmic slum, an inner-dimensional dead end. . . . Less fathomable are his memories of a moonlit corridor where mirrors scream and laugh, dark peaks of some kind that won't remain still, a stairway that's 'broken' in a very strange way . . ." (SDD, p. 13).

The book Victor Keirion finds in "Vastarien" is similar:

> It seemed to be a chronicle of strange dreams. Yet somehow

the passages he examined were less a recollection of unruled visions than a tangible incarnation of them, not mere rhetoric but the thing itself. The use of language in the book was arrantly unnatural and the book's author unknown. Indeed, the text conveyed the impression of speaking for itself and speaking only to itself, the words flowing together like shadows that were cast by no forms outside the book. But although this volume appeared to be composed in a vernacular of mysteries, its words did inspire a sure understanding and created in their reader a visceral apprehension of the world they described, existing inseparable from it. (SDD, p. 269)

It is not surprising, therefore, that Ligotti has written, in addition to the actual essay "The Consolations of Horror," several pseudo-essays on the writing of weird fiction. The most interesting of these is "Notes on the Writing of Horror: A Story." This work proposes to narrate a tale in three distinct styles—the realistic, the traditional Gothic, and the experimental. In the course of this disquisition it becomes clear where Ligotti's own sympathies lie. He dispenses with the realistic technique, viciously parodying the Stephen King style of mundane realism ("Nathan is a normal and real character, sure. . . . And to make him a bit more real, one could supply his coat, his car, and grandfather's wristwatch with specific brand names, perhaps autobiographically borrowed from one's own closet, garage, and wrist" [SDD, p. 105]). The traditional Gothic style is a little more to Ligotti's liking, but only because "isolated supernatural incidents don't look as silly in a Gothic tale as they do in a realistic one" (SDD, p. 108). One would imagine that the experimental technique is in fact Ligotti's own, but his lukewarm account of it makes this doubtful. Then we find a fourth technique, and it gains Ligotti's resounding vote of approval: ". . . the proper style of horror is really that of the *personal confession*" (SDD, p. 113). This connects with a sentiment in "The Consolations of Horror": "Nothing is worse than that which happens personally to a person" (43). This may be nothing more than the old adage that you can't frighten anyone else unless you yourself are frightened, but in some fashion or other it leads to the curious notion that "the tale teller, ideally, should himself be a writer of horror fiction by trade" (SDD, p. 114). The number of writers in

Ligotti's fiction is unusually high.

There are, of course, certain drawbacks to this extreme self-consciousness and awareness of the heritage of horror on Ligotti's part. I have already cited, in connection with Peter Straub, Peter Penzoldt's comment that Lovecraft "was too well read" (Penzoldt, p. 64), and I fear that criticism may apply even more aptly to Ligotti. The original edition of *Songs of a Dead Dreamer* contained some disastrous attempts at comic rewritings of classic horror tales—*The Island of Dr. Moreau, Dr. Jekyll and Mr. Hyde, Frankenstein*—which Ligotti wisely removed in the later edition. Elsewhere he has perpetrated still more arid and jejune rewritings of Poe ("Selections of Poe") and Lovecraft ("Selections of Lovecraft"). I am utterly at a loss to understand the purpose of these writings. Even a work such as "Studies in Horror"—a series of prose-poems or vignettes each narrated in a different style ("Transcendent Horror," "Gothic Horror," "Spectral Horror," etc.)—is certainly a tour de force of sorts and reveals Ligotti's mastery of these varied idioms, but the whole seems dry and academic. And a story like "The Mystics of Muelenberg" suffers from an attention to the niceties of language so excessive as to rob the words of their imagistic power. They don't add up to anything beyond themselves.

At this point I wish to make a brief digression to consider Ligotti's attitude to Lovecraft, since I believe it will enlighten us on his precise place in weird fiction. Ligotti has remarked: "I hope my stories are in the Lovecraftian tradition in that they may evoke a sense of terror whose source is something nightmarishly unreal, the implications of which are disturbingly weird and, in the magical sense, charming" (R, p. 21). But in explaining why he does not use the framework and nomenclature of Lovecraft's myth-cycle, Ligotti adds that "Lovecraft's universe . . . is a very specific model of reality, one whose portrayal demands a more realistic approach to fiction writing than mine is" (R, p. 21). The relatively tactful reference to realism is to be noted, since it contrasts violently with the snide attack on supernatural realism in "Notes on the Writing of Horror." And yet, Lovecraft was a supernatural realist, and the difference between him and the brand-name realism of Stephen King is a difference of methodology and not, fundamentally, one of approach. Ligotti has flatly declared that he is most attracted to

Lovecraft's early tales (F, p. 34; DM, p. 117), in which the dream element is more prevalent and the supernatural elements not always satisfactorily accounted for; he has remarked of the later work that "I find Lovecraft's fastidious attempts at creating a documentary style 'reality' an obstacle to appreciating his work" (F, p. 33). Two stories by Ligotti are markedly Lovecraftian: "The Sect of the Idiot" appears to be influenced most by "The Music of Erich Zann" and "The Festival"; "The Last Feast of Harlequin" (dedicated "To the memory of H. P. Lovecraft" [G, p. 45]) does indeed draw upon Lovecraft's late tale "The Shadow over Innsmouth" (but more perhaps upon "The Festival," Lovecraft's earlier working out of the same idea), but we shall see that this story is an extreme anomaly in Ligotti's fiction. In any event, a very crude distinction between Lovecraft and Ligotti might be enunciated as follows: whereas Lovecraft tries to make the unreal (i.e., the supernatural) real, Ligotti tries to make the real unreal (i.e., everything is "supernatural," or at any rate unnatural and monstrous).

Ligotti's emphasis on language has led him, like Lovecraft, to be very prodigal in the inventing of mythical books. *Vastarien, Cynothoglys, The Noctuary of Tine*—these are only a few of the cryptic volumes in the Ligottian library. The author has remarked: "I have some notes about the 'forbidden book,' in the Lovecraftian sense, that is, a kind of metaphysical obscenity, an offense against all conception of order. I think my conclusion was that the forbidden book would require the forbidden author to write it, though it might be a work of imagination and not, like the *Necronomicon,* a book of genuine revelation" (DM, p. 116). Imagination as opposed to revelation: here again is a critical distinction between the Ligottian and the Lovecraftian universe. Lovecraft's tomes reveal loathsome truths about the real world, Ligotti's transport one to the unreal.

"Vastarien" is Ligotti's most searching exploration of the forbidden book theme. The plot of this richly atmospheric tale—which stands with "The Last Feast of Harlequin" at the pinnacle of Ligotti's achievement—is deceptively simple: a man finds a book and it drives him mad. But what a wealth of dense imagery is created by means of this seemingly hackneyed device! Victor

Keirion searches for a book to transport him out of this world, but most of the "forbidden" books he finds are insufficient for the task: they are all "sodden with an obscene reality, falsely hermetic ventures which consisted of circling the same absurd landscape. The other worlds portrayed in these books inevitably served as annexes of this one; they were impostors of the authentic unreality which was the only realm of redemption, however gruesome it might appear" (SDD, p. 264-65). But *Vastarien* is different: it is "'not about something, but actually is that something'" (SDD, p. 267). This is a piquant conception, and a very neat resolution of the inveterate problem of the relation between the signifier and the signified—here they are one! But what sort of book is *Vastarien*? "To all appearances it seemed he had discovered the summit or abyss of the unreal, that paradise of exhaustion, confusion, and debris where reality ends and where one may dwell among its ruins" (SDD, p. 271). I shall return to this conception later.

Another extraordinarily powerful tale, "Nethescurial," strikes me as a very subtle—and perhaps unconscious—adaptation of Lovecraft's seminal story "The Call of Cthulhu." This is not to deny the essential originality of Ligotti's work, nor to suggest that the tale in any way incorporates the now hackneyed "Cthulhu Mythos" in the manner of an August Derleth or a Brian Lumley; but I believe that the basic framework of the two tales is strikingly similar. Lovecraft's tale is divided into three sections. In the first, a man discovers papers left by his grand-uncle attesting to the existence of a cult worshipping a hideous god, Cthulhu, and the possible existence of that entity itself; the second section narrates a policeman's discovery of this cult and its beliefs; the third section finally reveals—although again through a document—the actual existence of Cthulhu as he attacks the hapless crew of a derelict ship.

It can be seen that the basic pattern in Lovecraft's story is the gradual transformation of words into reality: whereas at the outset we only read of Cthulhu from the narrator's paraphrase of documents, at the end we vicariously experience the proximity of the nameless creature. Ligotti adapts this pattern and in a sense even surpasses it. "Nethescurial" is presented as a letter written by one friend to another; it begins: "I have uncovered a rather wonderful manuscript" (G, p. 69). This manuscript tells of a man who comes to a mysterious island named Nethescurial and, in the course of discussions with a Dr. N—, learns of an "omnipresent evil in the living world" (G, p. 71), "an absolute evil whose reality is mitigated only by our blindness to it" (G, p. 75). Suggestive as this is, the horrors remain curiously abstract; the letter-writer even remarks that the "words of this peculiar manuscript seem rather weak in this regard"—i.e., in the matter of actually conveying the bizarrerie of the situation. Thus ends the first section of the tale.

In the second section the letter-writer has experienced a disturbing dream in which he is in a room poring over maps, all of which feature some island named Nethescurial. In the room is an altar with an idol on it; when a weird band of worshippers comes to pray before it, one of the worshippers loathsomely melds with the idol.

The third section of the tale opens with the remark: "Well, it seems this letter has mutated into a chronicle of my adventures Nethescurialian" (G, p. 81). The writer speaks more truly than he knows, for as this section proceeds we learn that the writer's own words are insidiously being mutated by Nethescurial (whatever it may be), as he unwittingly begins to duplicate the expressions of the manuscript he had so desultorily examined at the outset. The relations to Lovecraft's story are obscure but significant—Nethescurial as a parallel for the sunken island of R'lyeh; worshippers praying before an entity whose true nature they themselves may not understand; Cthulhu's influence of dreams paralleled by the narrator's loss of control over his own language—and Ligotti brings home the reality of the weird phenomenon in a way that perhaps even exceeds Lovecraft: the letter-writer can only conclude with a pitiable denial of the true state of affairs, "I am not dying in a nightmare" (G, p. 84).

It is already evident that one vehicle by which the unreal is reached is dream. I have no doubt that many of Ligotti's tales incorporate fragments of his own dreams; but there is certainly more to it than that. Consider another comment on Lovecraft: "Lovecraft dreamed the great dream of supernatural literature—to convey with the greatest possible intensity a vision of the universe as a kind of enchanting nightmare" (F, p. 32). This, too, is clearly Ligotti's dream. It is suggestive that, in answering a query as to why he took to writing horror fiction, he noted: "I've never been tempted to write anything that was not essentially nightmarish" (F, p. 30)—as if horror and nightmare are fundamentally synonymous.

Ligotti's treatment of the dream theme is complex and multifarious. On occasion it can be very simple, as in "Oneiric Horror," an exquisite prose-poem that does nothing but paint a dream. I wonder whether, as with Dunsany's *Book of Wonder,* Ligotti wrote this vignette as a sort of elaboration or commentary on the illustration by Harry O. Morris, Jr., that accompanies it. In any event, the details and objects of this dream are described with all the meticulous realism that other writers would bestow upon the real world. A very suggestive phrase in "The Dream of a Mannikin" —"the divinity of the dream" (SDD, p. 56)—is capable of two meanings: in the surface plot of the story it refers to the sense of irrefutable reality a dream conveys to its dreamer for the duration of its existence; but it also suggests—again metafictionally—the dominance of dream over reality.

This dream-world or other realm (although recall that it is not an "other" realm but merely an aspect—perhaps the "true" aspect- of this realm) takes a peculiar form in Ligotti. We have already cited some characteristics of it: the "back alleys of some cosmic slum" in "The Frolic," the "paradise of exhaustion, confusion, and debris" in "Vastarien." Or consider the sinister movie theatre in "The Glamour": ". . . the round-backed seats were at the same time rows of headstones in a graveyard; the aisles were endless filthy alleys, long desolate corridors in an old asylum, or the dripping passages of a sewer narrowing into the distance; the pale movie screen was a dust-blinded window in a dark unvisited cellar, a mirror gone rheumy with age in an abandoned house; the chandelier and smaller fixtures were the facets of murky crystals embedded in the sticky walls of an unknown cavern" (G, p. 166). This notion of the world-as-junkheap is obsessively pervasive in Ligotti, and—although he himself merely states that this sort of imagery has "haunted me since childhood" (DM, p. 117)—I wonder whether it has to do with Ligotti's general world view: "Being something of a pessimist, I tend to think, in those rare moments when I really think, that existence is by nature evil. And nothing is good" (DM, p. 116). "Mad Night of Atonement," a rather tiresome and longwinded story, enunciates this idea. Dr. Francis Haxhausen, a sort of itinerant showman very much like Lovecraft's Nyarlathotep, has discovered the "law and the truth of the Creator": "what delight His heart" are "ruins and the ghosts of puppets": "'All the lonesome pathetic things, all the desolate dusty things, all the misbegotten things, ruined things, failed things, all the imperfect semblances and deteriorating remnants of what we arrogantly deign to call the Real, to call . . . Life. In brief, the entire realm of the unreal—wherein He abides—is what He loves like nothing in this world'" (N, p. 113). This is, I take it, what Robert M. Price has termed Ligotti's Gnostic vision the notion of the "imbecilic demiurge, a distant relation of the true divinity and the ill-advised creator of the dreadful material world" (Price, p. 29). Ligotti himself confirms this conception in "Nethescurial": "Imagine the universe as the dream, the feverish nightmare of a demonic demiurge" (G, p. 76). I wonder, too, whether the mannikin or puppet theme, which also recurs with great frequency in Ligotti's work, can be related to this idea. On the most elementary level the mannikin theme simply suggests a mockery of the human: Dr. Haxhausen can momentarily turn human beings into puppets, and perhaps vice versa, and at the end of the tale it appears that Haxhausen's audience—and perhaps the entire world—has been so transformed (or perhaps was so all along). On another level the notion relates to Ligotti's conception of characterization in weird fiction, as enunciated in "The Consolations of Horror." In discussing "The Fall of the House of Usher" Ligotti notes that we do not genuinely care about the fates of the human characters in the tale—our perspective as readers is more godlike: "This is a world created with built-in obsolescence, and to appreciate fully this downrunning cosmos one must take the perspective of its creator, which is all perspectives without getting sidetracked into a single one. . . . And the consolation in this is that we are supremely removed from the maddeningly tragic viewpoint of the human" ("Consolations," p. 47). I cannot help feeling that there is a strain of misanthropy running through Ligotti's work (I hardly need add that this is not meant pejoratively): the protagonist of "Alice's Last Adventure" remarks acidly, "Thank goodness there's only one of everybody" (SDD, p. 40). The clinical detachment of Ligotti's narrative voice, the sardonic (or, in his poorer work, cheaply sarcastic) tone he adopts in reference to his human puppets, and the number of characters who reveal themselves by their own words to be grotesque buffoons certainly underscore a refreshing scorn for human life.

Some of Ligotti's tales allow a little more of the observably real world than others, and a few of these are among his great successes. "The Frolic," an early and relatively conventional story, is still powerful for the visions of a lunatic that so hideously defy the inept rationalizations of a psychiatrist to account for them naturalistically. "Alice's Last Adventure" recounts a rather old idea—fictional characters coming to life—but does so with great adeptness and cumulative power. I could have done without the trite ending—the author, overtaken by her creations, scribbles away to the bitter end—and I also think that this tale is remarkably similar in conception to Jonathan Carroll's *The Land of Laughs* (1980), although perhaps the idea was probably not derived directly from that work.

"Les Fleurs" is emblematic of the "twisted or obscure technique" that Ligotti employs in his work. Here again the plot seems simple—a man evidently lures and kills a series of women—but a profound unease is engendered in the reader because of the many features of the story that are left tantalizingly unexplained. The protagonist has apparently already killed one woman, Clare (it is never explained how), and is now pursuing another one, Daisy. At his apartment he shows her an odd object that looks something like a cactus or perhaps a furry animal (the function of this object is never clarified). He attends meetings of some sort (their nature and purpose are never elucidated). Finally he shows her a painting, but her reaction is not what he was expecting: she is nonplussed and perhaps a little disturbed. And when we read that Daisy now "truly possesse[s] a sure knowledge of my secrets" (SDD, p. 26) and that her fate is accordingly sealed, we realize the truth (or, at least, a fragment of the truth): the man is not a mere homicidal maniac but one who wishes to indoctrinate a woman of the proper sensitivity into his mysterious sect, but who must kill any who are not suitable.

Incredibly, "The Last Feast of Harlequin" is a relatively early tale of Ligotti's (F, p. 34), and yet it is leagues away from the nightmarish unreality of the rest of his work. I trust it is not simply my bias toward supernatural realism that makes me rank this tale as Ligotti's best. If nothing else, it may perhaps be the very best homage to Lovecraft ever written. To call it a mere pastiche would be to do it an injustice.

The story follows traditional Lovecraftian lines: an anthropologist interested in exploring the "significance of the clown figure in diverse cultural contexts" (G, p. 3) reads an article by a former professor of his, Dr. Raymond Thoss (who, I take it, is not the same as the Dr. Thoss of "The Troubles of Dr. Thoss" [SDD, p. 155-67]), about a festival that takes place every year in December in the Midwestern town of Mirocaw. He visits the town in the summer and thinks he sees Dr. Thoss there, although he appears transformed into an inarticulate derelict. This compels him actually to go to the town during the festival. He insinuates himself into the goings-on, dresses up as one of the many derelicts who seem to serve some cryptic ritual function, is led by them into an underground chamber where horrors of various sorts transpire. This superficial and incomplete synopsis cannot even begin to suggest the tale's richness of texture, density of atmosphere, psychological and topographical realism, and—the most Lovecraftian feature of all—the notion of ancient and loathsome rituals surviving into the present day, related to and perhaps the origin of the most ancient human myth-cycles. If there is any complaint to be made of this story, it is that it appears to lack the cosmicism of Lovecraft's most representative work. The bulk of the story is very likely derived from Lovecraft's "The Festival" (1923), with a brief nod to "The Shadow over Innsmouth" at the end. The horror of the story seems to affect only random individuals rather than, as in the later Lovecraft, the entire race or the entire cosmos. Nevertheless, "The Last Feast of Harlequin" clearly demonstrates that Ligotti can write the sort of documentary realism he appears to scorn without losing the individuality of his own voice.

Ligotti's third collection, *Noctuary* (1994), reveals some disturbing features. In the first place, most of the stories are reprints, and Ligotti has seriously erred both in opening the volume with "The Medusa," which displays him at his worst in a long-winded tale full of self-indulgent, smart-alecky, high-sounding sentences that in the end mean nothing, and in closing it with an augmented version of the "Studies in Horror" (now collectively titled "Notebook of the Night"). It might be thought—given Ligotti's general scorn for the mechanics of plot and his emphasis on mood—that the prose-poem would be an ideal form for him, but it is exactly here that his single-minded emphasis on pure verbal witchery presents its greatest drawbacks. Ligotti has failed to note that even the most delicate prose-poems—whether by Baudelaire or Clark Ashton Smith or Dunsany (*Fifty-One Tales*)—must present some unified or coherent narrative if they are to have any effect. Most of these items are simply too insubstantial, fragmentary, and directionless to amount to much. A passage from "The Spectral Estate" typifies their essence: "Long exasperated by questions without answers, by answers without consequences, by truths which change nothing, we learn to become intoxicated by the mood of mystery itself, by the odor of the unknown. We are entranced by the subtle scents and wavering reflections of the unimaginable" (N 175-76). This is an ideal that Ligotti does not always fulfill; and most of these items, written with undeniable panache as they are, simply leave no impression upon the reader and are forgotten the moment they are finished.

The other disturbing thing about *Noctuary* is that there is only one original work in the volume; and yet, this tale, "The Tsalal," is almost worth all the other stories combined. It concerns an individual, Andrew Maness, who is the incarnation of the Tsalal (a term taken consciously from Poe's *Narrative of Arthur Gordon Pym*), or "a *perfect blackness*" (N 86). Maness's father, a reverend, has written a book called *Tsalal,* and Andrew ponders its significance:

> "'There is no nature to things,' you wrote in the book. 'There are no faces except masks held tight against the pitching chaos behind them.' You wrote that there is not true growth or evolu-

tion in the life of this world but only transformations of appearance, an incessant melting and molding of surfaces without underlying essence. Above all you pronounced that there is no salvation of any being because no beings exist as such, nothing exists to be saved—everything, everyone exists only to be drawn into the slow and endless swirling of mutations that we may see every second of our lives if we simply gaze through the eyes of the Tsalal." (N 80)

I do not know if this accurately represents Ligotti's philosophy, but it is an ideal instance of that *intellectualized horror* of which he is such a master. Somehow Andrew Maness is the embodiment of this nihilistic existentialism, and only Ligotti could have written so compellingly hypnotic a tale around such a dryly philosophical conception.

The fact that Ligotti has written (or published) so few new tales in the last few years is indeed a cause for worry, and one hopes that he is not prematurely "written out"; my feeling—perhaps it is only a hope—is that he is undergoing a fallow period while searching for something new to say, or a new way to say it. He has surely done all that one can possibly do in his current idiom. My respect for Ligotti is considerable: he has literary gifts beyond what most other writers in this field could even dream of; he has a uniqueness of vision that sets his work radically apart from all others; he is a highly articulate spokesman for his brand of weird fiction; and he has read exhaustively in the best work in the field and has profited enormously thereby. But I am troubled by a number of things: his writing is so self-conscious and self-referential that it utterly lacks spontaneity and emotional vigor; its appeal seems directed almost wholly to the intellect; he seems, apparently by design, not to care about the complete reconciliation of the various supernatural features in a given tale; and a number of his stories—like "The Shadow at the Bottom of the World" (G, p. 203-14), one of the most exquisitely modulated pieces of prose I have ever read—are flawlessly written by the sentence but do not in the end convey a very powerful impression. I fervently hope that Ligotti is not in danger—especially in light of the recent championing of his work by leading critics in the field—of becoming self-indulgent, overly obscure, and (worst of all) content to remain at the level he has attained. He will, I believe, have to start writing more stories—as opposed to the vignettes, prose poems, sketches, and fragments that so far constitute the bulk of his output—if he is to gain preëminence in the field. Ligotti's own tastes notwithstanding, few will doubt that Lovecraft initiated the most representative phase of his career when he adopted the documentary realism of "The Call of Cthulhu" in 1926; if he had stopped writing before that point, we would have little reason to remember him. This is not to say that Ligotti's current work is somehow qualitatively equal to Lovecraft's pre-1926 work (it is, in some ways, rather better); nor, of course, is it possible to say that "The Last Feast of Harlequin" is a harbinger for a realistic phase on Ligotti's part, since it is an early work. But I think that Ligotti will have to write more tales like "The Last Feast of Harlequin," "Vastarien," or "Nethescurial" if he is to join the ranks of Lovecraft, Blackwood, Dunsany, Jackson, Campbell, and Klein, as he is on the verge of doing.

WORKS CITED

Dziemianowicz, Stefan and Michael Morrison. "The Language of Dread: An Interview with Thomas Ligotti." *Science Fiction and Fantasy Book Review Annual 1990*, ed. Robert A. Collins and Robert Latham. Westport, CT: Greenwood Press, 1991, pp. 109-118. [Abbreviated in the text as DM.]

Eliot, T. S. "The Metaphysical Poets" (1921). In *Selected Essays*. New York: Harcourt, Brace, 1950.

Ford, Carl T. "Notes on the Writing of Horror: An Interview with Thomas Ligotti." *Dagon*, nos. 22/23 (Sept.-Dec. 1988): 30-35. [Abbreviated in the text as F.]

Lévy, Maurice. *Lovecraft: A Study in the Fantastic*. Trans. S. T. Joshi. Detroit: Wayne State University Press, 1988.

Ligotti, Thomas. "Allan and Adelaide: An Arabesque." *Crypt of Cthulhu* No. 68 (Hallowmass 1989): 10-16.

—————. "Charnelhouse of the Moon." *Crypt of Cthulhu* No. 68 (Hallowmass 1989): 35-36.

—————. "The Consolations of Horror." *Crypt of Cthulhu* No. 68 (Hallowmass 1989): 42-48.

—————. "Ghost Stories for the Dead." *Crypt of Cthulhu* No. 68 (Hallowmass 1989): 18-20.

—————. *Grimscribe: His Lives and Works.* London: Robinson, 1991. *New York: Carroll & Graf, 1991. [Abbreviated in the text as G.]

—————. *Noctuary.* London: Robinson, 1994. New York: Carroll & Graf, 1994. [Abbreviated in the text as N.]

—————. "Oneiric Horror." *Dagon* Nos. 22/23 (September-December 1988): 55-56.

—————. "The Real Wolf." *Nocturne* No. 1 (1988): 6-9.

—————. "A Selection of Poe." *Fantasy and Terror* No. 6 (1985): 20-24.

—————. "Selections of Lovecraft." *Crypt of Cthulhu* No. 68 (Hallowmass 1989): 38-41.

—————. *Songs of a Dead Dreamer.* 1986. Rev. ed. London: Robinson, 1989. [Abbreviated in the text as SDD.]

—————. "Ten Steps to Thin Mountain." *Crypt of Cthulhu* No. 68 (Hallowmass 1989): 37, 36.

Lovecraft, H. P. *The Annotated Supernatural Horror in Literature.* Edited by S. T. Joshi. New York: Hippocampus Press, 2000.

—————. *Selected Letters* 1929-1931. Edited by August Derleth and Donald Wandrei. Sauk City, WI: Arkham House, 1971.

—————. *Selected Letters* 1932-1934. Edited by August Derleth and James Turner. Sauk City, WI: Arkham House, 1976.

Penzoldt, Peter. *The Supernatural in Fiction.* 1952. Excerpts rpt. in *H. P. Lovecraft: Four Decades of Criticism,* ed. S. T. Joshi. Athens: Ohio University Press, 1980.

Price, Robert M. "Thomas Ligotti's Gnostic Quest." *Studies in Weird Fiction* No. 9 (Spring 1991): 27-31.

Ramsey, Shawn. "A Graveside Chat: An Interview with Thomas Ligotti." *Deathrealm* No. 8 (Spring 1989): 21-23. [Abbreviated in the text as R.]

THOMAS LIGOTTI: A BIBLIOGRAPHY

(22 October 2002)

Douglas A. Anderson

[Compiler's Note: This is a work-in-progress, but contains everything that I know about as of October 2002. Corrections and additions welcomed by the compiler at: nodens100@hotmail.com]

BOOKS, PAMPHLETS, AND BROADSIDES:

Songs of a Dead Dreamer.

- Albuquerque, NM: Silver Scarab Press, 1985 [trade paperback]

[300 copies in trade paperback. Illustrated by Harry O. Morris. Issued in March 1986. Note: some bibliographies, including a previous version of this one, state that the Silver Scarab Press edition was published in two forms, 250 copies in trade paperback, and 50 hardcovers. This hardcover edition is frequently rumored, though never seen, and the author himself has informed me that *"Dead Dreamer* came out in a 300-copy edition, all trade paperbacks." The book was apparently not published until March 1986. A printed postcard the publisher, announcing that the book is now available, has been observed bearing the postmark 25 March 1986.] [Contains eleven stories and seven sketches in four sections, plus introduction by Ramsey Campbell: "Introduction" by Ramsey Campbell; *Here and There*: "The Frolic; "Les Fleurs"; "Aunt Elise: A Tale of Possession in Old Grosse Pointe"; "Drink to Me Only with Labyrinthine Eyes"; "Alice's Last Aventure"; "Dream of a Mannikin, or the Third Person"; "The Troubles of Dr. Thoss"; *Elsewhere*: "Dr. Voke and Mr. Veech"; "The Greater Festival of Masks"; *Tales Retold*: "Three Scientists" ["One Thousand Painful Variations Performed upon Divers Creatures Undergoing the Treatment of Dr. Moreau, Humanist"; "The Excruciating Final Days of Dr. Henry Jekyll, Englishman"; and "The Agonizing Resurrection of Victor Frankenstein, Citizen of Geneva"]; "Two Immortals" ["The Heart of Count Dracula, Descendent of Attila, Scourge of God"; and "The Insufferable Salvation of Lawrence Talbot the Wolfman"]; "Leading Men" ["The Unbearable Rebirth of the Phantom of the Wax Museum"; and "The Intolerable Lesson of the Phantom of the Opera"]; *Nowhere*: "Professor Nobody's Little Lectures on Supernatural Horror"; "Notes on the Writing of Horror: A Story".]

Songs of a Dead Dreamer [revised and expanded]

- London: Robinson, [October] 1989 [trade paper]
- New York: Carroll & Graf, [May] 1990 [hardcover]
- New York: Carroll & Graf, [May] 1991 [mass market paperback]

[Contains twenty stories in three sections, with introduction by Ramsey Campbell (reprinted from 1985 edition): "Introduction" by Ramsey Campbell; *Dreams for Sleepwalkers*: "The Frolic"; "Les Fleurs"; "Alice's Last Adventure"; "Dream of a Mannikin"; *The Nyctalops Trilogy*: "The Chymist," "Drink to me Only with Labyrinthine Eyes," "Eye of the Lynx"; "Notes on the Writing of Horror"; *Dreams for Insomniacs*: "The Christmas Eves of Aunt Elise"; "The Lost Art of Twilight"; "The Troubles of Dr. Thoss"; "Masquerade of a Dead Sword"; "Dr. Voke and Mr. Veech"; "Professor Nobody's Little Lectures onSupernatural Horror"; *Dreams for the Dead*: "Dr. Locrian's Asylum"; "The Sect of the Idiot"; "The Greater Festival of Masks"; "The Music of the Moon"; "The Journal of J. P. Drapeau"; "Vastarien."]

Grimscribe: His Lives and Works

- London: Robinson, [December] 1991 [hardcover]
- New York: Carroll & Graf, [December] 1991 [hardcover]
- New York: Jove, [September] 1994 [mass market paperback]

[Contains thirteen stories in five sections, plus introduction: "Introduction"; *The Voice of the Damned*: "The Last Feast of Harlequin"; "The Spectacles in the Drawer"; "Flowers of the Abyss"; "Nethescurial"; *The Voice of the Demon*: "The Dreaming in Nortown"; "The Mystics of Muelenburg"; "In the Shadow of Another World"; "The Cocoons"; *The Voice of the Dreamer*: "The Night School"; "The Glamour"; *The Voice of the Child*: "The Library of Byzantium"; "Miss Plarr"; *The Voice of Our Name*: "The Shadow at the Bottom of the World."]

[Note: the entire contents of *Grimscribe*, save for the introduction, are reprinted (without section divisions) in *The Nightmare Factory*. Also, L.W. Currey's *Catalog 110* (Summer 1997) offered for sale a proof copy of the Robinson edition of *Grimscribe*, which includes a story, "Mrs. Rinaldi's Angel," dropped from the published version of the book, and replaced with two stories, "The Night School" and "The Glamour."]

Noctuary

- London: Robinson, [January] 1994 [hardcover]
- New York: Carroll & Graf, [January] 1994 [hardcover]
- New York: Carroll & Graf, [April] 1995 [trade paperback]

[Contains eight stories and nineteen sketches in three sections, plus foreword: [foreword:] "In the Night, In the Dark: A Note on the Appreciation of Weird Fiction"; *Part One: Studies in Shadow*: "The Medusa"; "Conversations in a Dead Language"; "The Prodigy of Dreams"; "Mrs. Rinaldi's Angel"; *Part Two: Discourse on Blackness*: "The Tsalal"; "Mad Night of Atonement"; "The Strange Design of Master Rignolo"; "The Voice in the Bones"; *Part Three: Notebook of the Night*: "The Master's Eyes Shining with Secrets"; "Salvation by Doom"; "New Faces in the City"; "Autumnal"; "One May Be Dreaming"; "Death without End"; "The Unfamiliar"; "The Career of Nightmares"; "The Physic"; "The Demon Man"; "The Puppet Masters"; "The Spectral Estate"; "Primordial Loathing"; "The Nameless Horror"; "Invocation to the Void"; "The Mocking Mystery"; "The Interminable Equation"; "The Eternal Mirage"; "The Order of Illusion."]

The Agonizing Resurrection of Victor Frankenstein & Other Gothic Tales

- Eugene, OR: Silver Salamander Press, [October] 1994 [trade paperback of 1000 copies, hardcover limited to 140 copies, black leather edition limited to 40 copies, with an additional 10 presentation copies in red leather]

[Contains nineteen sketches in eight sections, plus introduction by Michael Shea: "Good-Tom-Go-Lightly" [verse, introduction] by Michael Shea; *Three Scientists*: "One Thousand Painful Variations Performed upon Divers Creatures Undergoing the Treatment of Dr. Moreau, Humanist"; "The Excruciating Final Days of Dr. Henry Jekyll, Englishman"; "The Agonizing Resurrection of Victor Frankenstein, Citizen of Geneva"; *Two Immortals*: "The Heart of Dracula, Descendent of Attila, Scourge of God"; "The Insufferable Salvation of Lawrence Talbot the Wolfman"; *Leading Men*: "The Intolerable Lesson of the Phantom of the Opera"; "The Unbearable Rebirth of the Phantom of the Wax Museum"; *Gothic Heroines*: "The Perilous Legacy of Emily St. Aubert, Inheritress of Udolpho"; "The Eternal Devotion of the Governess to the Residents of Bly"; *Loners*: "The Unnatural Persecution, by a Vampire, of Mr. Jacob J."; "The Superb Companion of Andre de V., Anti-Pygmalion"; "*Shut-Ins*: The Ever-Vigilant Guardians of Secluded Estates"; "The Scream: From 1800 to the Present"; *A Poe Anthology*: "The Transparent Alias of William Wilson, Sportsman and Scoundrel"; "The Worthy Inmate of the Will of the Lady Ligeia"; "The Interminable Residence of the Friends of the House of Usher"; *The Works & Death of H. P. Lovecraft*: "The Fabulous Alienation of the Outsider, Being of No Fixed Abode"; "The Blasphemous Enlightenment of Prof. Francis Wayland Thurston of Boston, Providence, and the Human Race"; "The Premature Death of H. P. Lovecraft, Oldest Man in New England".]

The Nightmare Factory
- London: Raven, [c. June] 1996 [trade paperback]
- New York: Carroll & Graf, [June] 1996 [trade paperback]

[Contains forty-five stories in four sections, plus introduction and foreword by Poppy Z. Brite: "Foreword" by Poppy Z. Brite; "Introduction: The Consolations of Horror"; *"Part 1: from Songs of a Dead Dreamer"*: "The Frolic"; "Les Fleurs"; "Alice's Last Adventure"; "Dream of a Mannikin"; "The Chymist"; "Drink to Me Only with Labyrinthine Eyes"; "Eye of the Lynx"; "The Christmas Eves of Aunt Elise"; "The Lost Art of Twilight"; "The Troubles of Dr. Thoss"; "Masquerade of a Dead Sword"; "Dr. Voke and Mr. Veech"; "Dr. Locrian's Asylum"; "The Sect of the Idiot"; "The Greater Festival of Masks"; "The Music of the Moon"; "The Journal of J. P. Drapeau"; "Vastarien"; Part 2: "Grimscribe": "The Last Feast of Harlequin"; "The Spectacles in the Drawer"; "Flowers of the Abyss"; "Nethescurial"; "The Dreaming in Nortown"; "The Mystics of Muelenburg"; "In the Shadow of Another World"; "The Cocoons"; "The Night School"; "The Glamour"; "The Library of Byzantium"; "Miss Plarr"; "The Shadow at the Bottom of the World"; Part 3: from "Noctuary": "The Medusa"; "Conversations in a Dead Language"; "The Prodigy of Dreams"; "Mrs. Rinaldi's Angel"; "The Tsalal"; "Mad Night of Atonement"; "The Strange Designs of Master Rignolo"; "The Voice in the Bones"; Part 4: "Teatro Grottesco and Other Tales": "Teatro Grottesco"; "Severini"; "Gas Station Carnivals"; "The Bungalow House"; "The Clown Puppet"; "The Red Tower."]

In a Foreign Town, In a Foreign Land
- London: Durtro, [August] 1997 [shrink-wrapped hardcover with CD by Current 93, published in an edition of 1000 copies. 60 additional copies were produced with marbled end-papers, and a small card autographed by Ligotti, Steven Stapleton (artist), David Tibet and Cristoph Heemann (musicians).]

- London: Durtro, [March] 2002 [reissued as a digipack with booklet]

[Contains four stories: "His Shadow Shall Rise to a Higher House"; "The Bells Will Sound Forever"; "A Soft Voice Whispers Nothing"; "When You Hear Singing, You Will Know It Is Time."]

I Have a Special Plan for This World [verse]
* London: Durtro, [April] 2000 [wrappers, limited to 125 numbered copies, frontispiece by Steven Stapledon, all copies signed by the author and the artist, printed by The Tragara Press.]

[Note: There are a few small textual differences from the Current 93 recording of the same title.]

This Degenerate Little Town [verse]
* London: Durtro, [September] 2001 [wrappers, limited to 160 copies, of which 120 are for sale; frontispiece by David Tibet, all copies signed by the author and the artist, printed by The Tragara Press. Each copy is accompanied by a compact disc containing a reading of the text by the author.]

What Good Is Your Head [verse]
* [Merion Station, PA]: [Jason Van Hollander], [March] 2002 [broadside] [Illustrated in color by Jason Van Hollander; numbered and signed by the author and illustrator. Limited to 350 copies.]

[one of a series of "Three Things They Will Never Tell You"]

My Work Is Not Yet Done: Three Tales of Corporate Horror
* Poplar Bluff, MO: Mythos Books, [July] 2002 [Limited to 1000 unnumbered hardcover copies. Frontispiece and dust-wrapper art by Harry O. Morris. Issued with a tipped in adhesive printed label, also designed by Morris, signed by the author and the artist.] [Contains three stories, each with a divisional title: I. *The Wages of Life*: "My Work Is Not Yet Done"; II. *The Second Coming of the Dead*: "I Have a Special Plan for This World" [short story]; and III. *Going Out of Business*: "The Nightmare Network."]

FORTHCOMING, AS OF OCTOBER 2002 (LISTED ALPHABETICALLY):

Crampton [screenplay, with Brandon Trenz]
* London: Durtro, [forthcoming 2002-2003]

[To be issued with a CD, entitled *The Unholy City*, containing a six-poem cycle inspired by the screenplay, written and recorded by

Ligotti.]

Sideshow and Other Stories [short story]

- Burton, MI: Subterranean Press, [forthcoming, planned for late 2002] [Illustrated by Jennifer Gariepy. Limited to 350 signed and numbered softcover chapbooks, and 52 signed and lettered hardcover copies.]

Some Things They Will Never Tell You [verse]

- London: Durtro, [forthcoming]

Teatro Grotesco

- London: Durtro, [forthcoming]

  [Planned to contain: "Teatro Grottesco"; "Severini"; "Gas Station Carnivals"; "The Bungalow House"; "The Clown Puppet"; "The Red Tower"; "The Shadow, The Darkness"; "Our Temporary Supervisor"; "My Case for Retributive Action;" "sideshow and Other Stories"; *In a Foreign Town, In a Foreign Land* [collective title of the next four stories]: "His Shadow Shall Rise to a Higher House"; "The Bells Will Sound Forever"; "A Soft Voice Whispers Nothing"; "When You Hear Singing, You Will Know It Is Time"; "I Have a Special Plan for This World" [verse]; "This Degenerate Little Town" [verse], "Paradoxes from Hell."]

What Becomes of the Body [verse]

- [Merion Station, PA]: [Jason Van Hollander], [forthcoming 2003] [broadside] [Illustrated in color by Jason Van Hollander; numbered and signed by the author and illustrator. Limited to 350 copies.]

  [one of a series of "Three Things They Will Never Tell You"]

What Happens to Faces [verse]

- [Merion Station, PA]: [Jason Van Hollander], [forthcoming 2003] [broadside] [Illustrated in color by Jason Van Hollander; numbered and signed by the author and illustrator. Limited to 350 copies.]

  [one of a series of "Three Things They Will Never Tell You"]

STORIES, VERSE AND SCREENPLAYS:

"The Agonizing Resurrection of Victor Frankenstein, Citizen of Geneva" *[sk]*

- *Songs of a Dead Dreamer* (1985) [under "Three Scientists"]

- *The Agonizing Resurrection of Victor Frankenstein & Other Gothic Tales* (1997)

"Alice's Last Adventure"

- *Songs of a Dead Dreamer* (1985)
- *Prime Evil* (1988) Douglas Winter (ed).
- *Songs of a Dead Dreamer* (revised, 1989)
- *The Nightmare Factory* (1996)

"Allan and Adelaide: An Arabesque"

- *Fantasy Macabre*, no. 2 (April 1981)
- *Crypt of Cthulhu*, 9 no. 1, whole no. 68 (Hallowmas 1989)

"Aunt Elise: A Tale of Possession in Old Grosse Point" *[see "The Christmas Eves of Aunt Elise"]*

"Autumn Horror" *[see "Autumnal"]*

"Autumnal" *[sk]*

- *Dagon*, no. 22/23 (September-December 1988) [as "Autumn Horror"]
- *Noctuary* (1994)

"The Bells Will Sound Forever"

- *In a Foreign Town, In a Foreign Land* (1997)
- Stephen Jones (ed.). *The Mammoth Book of Best New Horror*, v. 9 (1998)
- *Teatro Grotesco* (forthcoming)

"The Blasphemous Enlightenment of Prof. Francis Wayland Thurston of Boston, Providence, and the Human Race" *[sk]*

- *Fantasy & Terror*, no. 5 (1985) [part of "Selections of Lovecraft," with the name in the title given as "Prof. Angell"]
- Crypt of Cthulhu, 9 no. 1, whole no. 68 (Hallowmas 1989) [part of "selections of Lovecraft"]
- *The Agonizing Resurrection of Victor Frankenstein & Other Gothic Tales* (1997)

"The Bungalow House"

- *The Urbanite*, no. 5 (1995)
- *The Nightmare Factory* (1996)
- Stephen Jones (ed). *The Mammoth Book of Best New Horror, v. 7* (1996)
- *Teatro Grotesco* (forthcoming)

"The Career of Nightmares" *[sk]*

- *Tiamet*, no 5 (June/July 1991) [as "Nightmare Horror"]

- *Crypt of Cthulhu*, 9 no. 1, whole no. 68 (Hallowmas 1989) [as "Nightmare Horror," part of "Studies in Horror"]
- *Noctuary* (1994)

"Charnel House of the Moon"

- *Punk-Surrealist Cafe*, no. 6 (October 1981)
- *Crypt of Cthulhu*, 9 no. 1, whole no. 68 (Hallowmas 1989)

"The Christmas Eves of Aunt Elise: A Tale of Possession in Old Grosse Pointe"

- *Grimoire*, no. 3 (Winter 1982-1983)
- *Songs of a Dead Dreamer* (1985) [as "Aunt Elise: A Tale of Possession in Old Grosse Pointe"]
- *Songs of a Dead Dreamer* (revised, 1989)
- *The Nightmare Factory* (1996)

"The Chymist"

- *Nyctalops*, 3 no. 2, whole no. 16 (March 1981)
- *Songs of a Dead Dreamer* (revised, 1989)
- *The Nightmare Factory* (1996)

"The Clown Puppet"

- *The Nightmare Factory* (1996)
- *Teatro Grotesco* (forthcoming)

"The Cocoons"

- *Grimscribe* (1991)
- *Weird Tales*, 53 no. 2, whole no. 303 (Winter 1991-1992)
- *DAC News*, October 1992
- *The Nightmare Factory* (1996)

"The Complete Madman" *(sk) [collected in "Paradoxes from Hell," op. cit.]*

- *Grimoire*, no. 4 (1983) [under the pseudonym Charles Miguel Riaz]

"Conversations in a Dead Language"

- *Deathrealm*, No. 8 (Spring 1989)
- *Noctuary* (1994)
- *The Nightmare Factory* (1996)
- Richard Chizmar and Robert Morrish (eds.). *October Dreams* (2000)

"Crampton" *[by Thomas Ligotti and Brandon Trenz] [Unproduced screenplay written 1998, for an episode of* The X-Files*]*

- [posted at Thomas Ligotti Online 2000-2002]

- *Crampton* (forthcoming)

"Death without End" *[sk]*
- *Tiamet*, no 5 (June/July 1991) [as "Macabre Horror"]
- *Crypt of Cthulhu*, 9 no. 1, whole no. 68 (Hallowmas 1989) [as "Macabre Horror," part of "Studies in Horror"]
- *Noctuary* (1994)

"The Decayed Mystic" *[sk] [collected in "Paradoxes from Hell," op. cit.]*
- *Grimoire*, no. 4 (1983) [under the pseudonym Charles Miguel Riaz]

"The Demon Man" *[sk]*
- *Crypt of Cthulhu*, 9 no. 1, whole no. 68 (Hallowmas 1989) [as "Demonic Horror," part of "Studies in Horror"]
- *Noctuary* (1994)

"Demonic Horror" *[see "The Demon Man"]*

"The Deranged Poet" *(sk) [collected in "Paradoxes from Hell," op. cit.]*
- *Grimoire*, no. 4 (1983) [under the pseudonym Charles Miguel Riaz]

"Dr. Locrian's Asylum"
- *Grue*, no. 5 (1987)
- *Songs of a Dead Dreamer* (revised, 1989)
- *The Nightmare Factory* (1996)
- [posted at Thomas Ligotti Online (1998-2002)]

"Dr. Voke and Mr. Veech"
- *Grimoire*, no. 5 (Summer 1983)
- *Songs of a Dead Dreamer* (1985)
- *Songs of a Dead Dreamer* (revised, 1989)
- *The Nightmare Factory* (1996)
- [posted at Thomas Ligotti Online (1998-2002)]

"Dream of a Mannikin"
- *Eldritch Tales*, 2 no. 3, whole no. 9 (1982) [as "Dream of a Mannikin, or the Third Person"]
- *Songs of a Dead Dreamer* (1985) [as "Dream of a Mannikin, or the Third Person"]
- Jessica Amanda Salmonson (ed). *Tales by Moonlight II* (1989) [as "Dream of a Mannikin, or the Third Person"]
- *Songs of a Dead Dreamer* (revised, 1989)

- Dziemianowicz (et al, eds). *To Sleep, Perchance to Dream Nightmare* (1993)
- *The Nightmare Factory* (1996)

"The Dreaming in Nortown"

- *Tiamet*, no. 5 (June/July 1991)
- *Grimscribe* (1991)
- *The Nightmare Factory* (1996)

"Dreamworld Horror" *[see "The Eternal Mirage"]*

"Drink to Me Only with Labyrinthine Eyes"

- *Nyctalops*, 3 no. 3, whole no. 17 (June 1982)
- *Songs of a Dead Dreamer* (1985)
- *Songs of a Dead Dreamer* (revised, 1989)
- *The Nightmare Factory* (1996)

"The Dwarf" *[sk] by Aloysius Bertrand, translated by Thomas Ligotti*

- *Fantasy & Terror*, no. 6 (1985)

"The Eternal Devotion of the Governess to the Residents of Bly" *[sk]*

- *Fantasy & Terror*, no. 7 (1985)
- *The Agonizing Resurrection of Victor Frankenstein & Other Gothic Tales* (1997)

"The Eternal Mirage" *[sk]*

- *Tiamet*, no 5 (June/July 1991) [as "Dreamworld Horror"]
- *Crypt of Cthulhu*, 9 no. 1, whole no. 68 (Hallowmas 1989) [as "Dreamworld Horror," part of "Studies in Horror"]
  Noctuary (1994)

"The Ever-Vigilant Guardians of Secluded Estates" *[sk]*

- *Fantasy & Terror*, no. 7 (1985) [as "The Ever Vigilant Guardians of Secluded and Opulent Estates"]
- *The Agonizing Resurrection of Victor Frankenstein & Other Gothic Tales* (1997)

"Excerpt from Dreams of the Zodiac" *[see "The Physic"]*

"The Excruciating Final Days of Dr. Henry Jekyll, Englishman" *[sk]*

- *Songs of a Dead Dreamer* (1985) [under "Three Scientists"]
- *The Agonizing Resurrection of Victor Frankenstein & Other Gothic Tales* (1997)

"Exotic Horror" *[see "The Unfamiliar"]*

"Eye of the Lynx"

- *Nyctalops*, 3 no. 4, whole no. 18 (April 1983)
- *Songs of a Dead Dreamer* (revised, 1989)
- Michele Slung (ed). *Shudder Again* (1993)
- *The Nightmare Factory* (1996)

"The Fabulous Alienation of the Outsider, Being of No Fixed Abode" *[sk]*

- *Fantasy & Terror*, no. 5 (1985) [part of "selections of Lovecraft"]
- *Crypt of Cthulhu*, 9 no. 1, whole no. 68 (Hallowmas 1989) [part of 'selections of Lovecraft"]
- *The Agonizing Resurrection of Victor Frankenstein & Other Gothic Tales* (1997)

"Les Fleurs"

- *Dark Horizons*, no. 23 (Summer 1981)
- *Songs of a Dead Dreamer* (1985)
- *Songs of a Dead Dreamer* (revised, 1989)
- *The Nightmare Factory* (1996)

"Flowers of the Abyss"

- *Nyctalops*, 4 no. 1, whole no. 19 (April 1991)
- *Grimscribe* (1991)
- *The Nightmare Factory* (1996)

"The Frolic"

- *Fantasy Tales*, 5, whole no. 9 (Spring 1982)
- *Songs of a Dead Dreamer* (1985)
- Stephen Jones and David A. Sutton (eds). *The Best Horror from Fantasy Tales* (1988)
- *Songs of a Dead Dreamer* (revised, 1989)
- Stefan R. Dziemianowicz, Robert Weinberg and Martin H. Greenberg (eds), *Nursery Crimes* (1993)
- *The Nightmare Factory* (1996)

"Gas Station Carnivals"

- *The Nightmare Factory* (1996)
- Stephen Jones (ed). *The Best New Horror: Volume Eight* (1997)
- *Teatro Grotesco* (forthcoming)

"Ghost Stories for the Dead" *["The New Blackness"; "The New Silence"; "The Old Nonsense and the New"; "Tales of the New Dream"]*

- *Grimoire*, no. 2 (Fall 1982)
- *Crypt of Cthulhu*, 9 no. 1, whole no. 68 (Hallowmas 1989)
- [posted at Thomas Ligotti Online (1998-2002)]

"The Glamour"

- *Grimscribe* (1991)
- Brian M. Stableford (ed). *The Dedalus Book of Femme Fatales* (1992)
- Ellen Datlow and Terri Windling (eds). *Year's Best Fantasy & Horror: Fifth Annual Collection* (1992)
- Stephen Jones and Ramsey Campbell (eds). *Best New Horror 4* (1993)
- *The Nightmare Factory* (1996)

"Gothic Horror" *[see "Salvation by Doom"]*

"The Greater Festival of Masks"

- *Songs of a Dead Dreamer* (1985)
- Ramsey Campbell (ed). *Fine Frights: Stories That Scared Me* (1988)
- *Songs of a Dead Dreamer* (revised, 1989)
- *The Nightmare Factory* (1996)
- Robert Weinberg, Stefan R. Dziemianowicz, and Martin H. Greenberg (eds). *100 Tiny Tales of Terror* (1996)
- [posted at Thomas Ligotti Online (1998-2002)]

"The Heart of Count Dracula, Descendent of Attila, Scourge of God" *[sk]*

- *Songs of a Dead Dreamer* (1985) [under "Two Immortals"]
- *The Agonizing Resurrection of Victor Frankenstein & Other Gothic Tales* (1997)
- Robert Weinberg, Stefan R. Dziemianowicz, and Martin H. Greenberg (eds). *100 Vicious Little Vampire Stories* (1995)
- *Stephen Jones (ed). The Mammoth Book of Dracula* (1997)

"His Shadow Shall Rise to a Higher House"

- *In a Foreign Town, In a Foreign Land* (1997)
- *Weird Tales*, no. 315 ([January] 1999)
- *Teatro Grotesco* (forthcoming)

"I Have a Special Plan for This World" *[short story]*

- *Horror Garage #2* (November 2000)
- Stephen Jones, ed. *The Mammoth Book of Best New Horror, v. 12* (2001)
- *My Work Is Not Yet Done* (2002)

"I Have a Special Plan for This World" *[verse]*

- *I Have a Special Plan for This World* (2000)
- *Teatro Grotesco* (forthcoming)

"In a Foreign Land, In a Foreign Town" *[four stories]*

- *In a Foreign Land, In a Foreign Town* (1997)
- *Teatro Grotesco* (forthcoming)

"In the Shadow of Another World"

- *Dagon*, no. 21 (1988)
- *Grimscribe* (1991)
- *The Nightmare Factory* (1996)

"The Insufferable Salvation of Lawrence Talbot the Wolfman" *[sk]*

- *Songs of a Dead Dreamer* (1985) [under "Two Immortals"]
- *The Agonizing Resurrection of Victor Frankenstein & Other Gothic Tales* (1997)

"The Interminable Equation" *[sk]*

- *Tiamet*, no 5 (June/July 1991) [as "Nihilistic Horror"]
- *Crypt of Cthulhu*, 9 no. 1, whole no. 68 (Hallowmas 1989) [as "Nihilistic Horror," part of 'Studies in Horror"]
- *Noctuary* (1994)

"The Interminable Residence of the Friends of the House of Usher" *[sk]*

- *Fantasy & Terror*, no. 6 (1985) [part of "A Selection of Poe"]
- *The Agonizing Resurrection of Victor Frankenstein & Other Gothic Tales* (1997)

"The Intolerable Lesson of the Phantom of the Opera" *[sk]*

- *Songs of a Dead Dreamer* (1985) [under "Leading Men"]
- *The Agonizing Resurrection of Victor Frankenstein & Other Gothic Tales* (1997)

"Introduction" [to *Grimscribe*]

- *Grimscribe* (1991)

"Invocation to the Void" *[sk]*

- *Grimoire, no.* 6 (1983) [as "To Conceive of Another World," under the pseudonym Charles Miguel Riaz]
- *Crypt of Cthulhu*, 9 no. 1, whole no. 68 (Hallowmas 1989) [as "Occult Horror," part of 'Studies in Horror"]
- *Noctuary* (1994)

"The Journal of J. P. Drapeau"

- *Dagon*, no. 20 (1987)
- *Songs of a Dead Dreamer* (revised, 1989)
- [reworked into a scenario "In a City of Bells and Towers," as by

Mark Morrison and Thomas Ligotti, for the *Horror on the Orient-Express* gaming module for the 5th edition of *Call of Cthulhu* (1991)]

- *The Nightmare Factory* (1996)

"The Last Feast of Harlequin"

- *The Magazine of Fantasy & Science Fiction*, April 1990 [cover story]
- *Grimscribe* (1991)
- Ellen Datlow and Terri Windling (eds). *Year's Best Fantasy & Horror: Fourth Annual Collection* (1991)
- Stephen Jones and Ramsey Campbell (eds). *Best New Horror 2* (1991)
- Stephen Jones and Ramsey Campbell (eds). *The Giant Book of Best New Horror* (1993)
- Edward L. Ferman & Kristine Kathryn Rusch (eds). *The Best from Fantasy & Science Fiction: A 45th Anniversary Anthology* (1994)
- Jim Turner (ed). *Cthulhu 2000* (1995)
- *The Nightmare Factory* (1996)
- Joyce Carol Oates (ed). *American Gothic Tales* (1996)

"The Last Feast of Harlequin" [by Thomas Ligotti and Brandon Trenz]

- [Unpublished, unproduced screenplay based on Ligotti's short story of the same name (written 1999-2000).]

"Leading Men" *["The Unbearable Rebirth of the Phantom of the Wax Museum"; and "The Intolerable Lesson of the Phantom of the Opera"; see under individual titles]*

"The Library of Byzantium"

- *Dagon*, no. 22/23 (September-December 1988)
- *Grimscribe* (1991)
- *The Nightmare Factory* (1996)

"The Lost Art of Twilight"

- *Dark Horizon*, no. 30 (Summer 1986)
- *Songs of a Dead Dreamer* (revised, 1989)
- *Weird Tales*, no. 297 (Summer 1990)
- Martin H. Greenberg, Stefan R. Dziemianowicz and Robert Weinberg (eds). *A Taste for Blood* (1993)
- John Betancourt (ed). *Best of Weird Tales* (1995)
- *The Nightmare Factory* (1996)

"Macabre Horror" *[see "Death without End"]*

"Mad Night of Atonement"

- *Grue*, No. 9 (1989)
- *Noctuary* (1994)
- *The Nightmare Factory* (1996)

"The Madman," *by Aloysius Bertrand, translated by Thomas Ligotti*

- *Fantasy and Terror*, no. 7 (1985)

"Masquerade of a Dead Sword"

- Jessica Amanda Salmonson (ed). *Heroic Visions II* (1986)
- *Songs of a Dead Dreamer* (revised, 1989)
- *The Nightmare Factory* (1996)

"The Masters Eyes Shining with Secrets" *[sk]*

- *Fantasy & Terror*, no. 4 (1984) [as "Transcendental Horror"]
- *Crypt of Cthulhu*, 9 no. 1, whole no. 68 (Hallowmas 1989) [as "Transcendental Horror," part of "Studies in Horror"]
- *Noctuary* (1994)

"The Mechanical Museum" *[by John B. Ford and Thomas Ligotti]*

- John B. Ford and others. *The Evil Entwines* (forthcoming 2002)

"The Medusa"

- *Fantasy Tales*, 3 no. 1, whole no. 7 (Winter 1991)
- Stephen Jones and Ramsey Campbell (eds). *Best New Horror 3* (1992)
- Stephen Jones and Ramsey Campbell (eds). *The Giant Book of Terror* (1994)
- *Noctuary* (1994)
- Stephen Jones and David Sutton (eds). *The Giant Book of Fantasy Tales* (1996)
- *The Nightmare Factory* (1996)

"Miss Plarr"

- *Grimscribe* (1991)
- *Weird Tales*, 53 no. 2, whole no. 303 (Winter 1991-1992)
- *The Nightmare Factory* (1996)

"The Mocking Mystery" *[sk]*

- *Noctuary* (1994)

"Mrs. Rinaldi's Angel"

- Ellen Datlow (ed). A Whisper of Blood (1991)
- *Noctuary* (1994)
- *The Nightmare Factory* (1996)

"The Murderer," *by Gaston Danville, translated by Thomas Ligotti*

- *Fantasy Macabre*, no. 7 (1985)

"The Music of the Moon"

- *Fantasy Macabre*, no. 9 (1987)
- *Songs of a Dead Dreamer* (revised, 1989)
- *The Nightmare Factory* (1996)
- Stefan R. Dziemianowicz, Robert Weinberg and Martin H. Greenberg (eds). *100 Twisted Little Tales of Torment* (1998)

"My Case for Retributive Action"

- *Weird Tales*, 57 no. 4, whole no. 324 (Summer 2001)
- *Teatro Grotesco* (forthcoming)

"My Work Is Not Yet Done"

- [posted at *Thomas Ligotti Online*, January 2002]
- *My Work Is Not Yet Done* (2002)

"The Mystics of Muelenburg"

- *Crypt of Cthulhu*, 7 no. 1, whole no. 51 (Hallowmas 1987)
- *Grimscribe* (1991)
- *The Nightmare Factory* (1996)
- Stefan R. Dziemianowicz, Robert Weinberg and Martin H. Greenberg (eds). *100 Fiendish Little Frightmares* (1997)

"The Nameless Horror" *[sk]*

- *Crypt of Cthulhu*, 9 no. 1, whole no. 68 (Hallowmas 1989) [as "Nameless Horror," part of "Studies in Horror"]
- *Noctuary* (1994)

"Nethescurial"

- *Grimscribe* (1991)
- *Weird Tales*, 53 no. 2, whole no. 303 (Winter 1991-1992)
- *The Nightmare Factory* (1996)

"The New Blackness" *[sk] [see "Ghost Stories for the Dead"]*

"New Faces in the City" *[sk]*

- *Crypt of Cthulhu*, 9 no. 1, whole no. 68 (Hallowmas 1989) [as "Unreal Horror," part of 'Studies in Horror"]
- *Noctuary* (1994)

"The New Silence" *[sk] [see "Ghost Stories for the Dead"]*

"The Night School"

- *Grimscribe* (1991)
- *Tekeli-li!*, no. 4 (Winter/Spring 1992)

- *The Nightmare Factory* (1996)

"Nightmare Horror" *[see "The Career of Nightmares"]*

"The Nightmare Network"

- John C. Pelan (ed). *Darkside: Horror for the Next Millenium* (1996)
- *Esoterra*, no. 8 (Winter/Spring 1999)
- *My Work Is Not Yet Done* (2002)

"Nihilistic Horror" *[see "The Interminable Equation"]*

"Notes on the Writing of Horror: A Story"

- *Dark Horizons*, no. 28 (Spring 1985)
- *Songs of a Dead Dreamer* (1985)
- *Songs of a Dead Dreamer* (revised, 1989)
- David G. Hartwell (ed). *Foundations of Fear* (1992)
- David G. Hartwell (ed). *Foundations of Fear: Visions of Fear* (1994)

"The Nyctalops Trilogy" ["The Chymist"; "Drink to Me Only with Labyrinthine Eyes"; and "Eye of the Lynx"; these three stories are referred to as "The Nyctalops Trilogy" only on the contents page of the expanded *Songs of a Dead Dreamer* (1989)]

"Occult Horror" *[see "Invocation to the Void"]*

"The Old Nonsense and the New" *[sk] [see "Ghost Stories for the Dead"]*

"One May Be Dreaming" *[sk]*

- *Dagon*, no. 22/23 (September-December 1988) [as "Oneiric Horror"]
- *Noctuary* (1994)

"One Thousand Painful Variations Performed upon Divers Creatures Undergoing the Treatment of Dr. Moreau, Humanist" *[sk]*

- *Grimoire*, no. 1 (Summer 1982)
- *Songs of a Dead Dreamer* (1985) [under "Three Scientists"]
- *Rhysling Anthology 1986*
- *The Agonizing Resurrection of Victor Frankenstein & Other Gothic Tales* (1997)

"Oneiric Horror" *[see "One May Be Dreaming"]*

"The Order of Illusion" *[sk]*

- *Fantasy & Terror*, no. 4 (1984) [*Twelve Ghosts and Twelve Others*] [as "Order of Illusion"]
- *Crypt of Cthulhu*, 9 no. 1, whole no. 68 (Hallowmas 1989) [as "Or-

der of Illusion"]

- *Noctuary* (1994)

"Our Temporary Supervisor"

- *Weird Tales*, 58 no. 1, whole no. 325 (Fall 2001)
- Stephen Jones, ed. *The Mammoth Book of Best New Horror, v. 13* (2002)
- *Teatro Grotesco* (forthcoming)

"Paradoxes from Hell" *[a grouping of five short pieces: "The Decayed Mystic"; "The Stricken Philosopher"; "The Deranged Poet"; "The Complete Madman"; and "Postscript"]*

- *AKLO: A Volume of the Fantastic*, edited by Mark Valentine, Roger Dobson and R.B. Russell (1998)
- *Teatro Grotesco* (forthcoming)

"The Perilous Legacy of Emily St. Aubert, Inheritress of Udolpho" *[sk]*

- *Fantasy & Terror*, no. 7 (1985)
- *The Agonizing Resurrection of Victor Frankenstein & Other Gothic Tales* (1997)

"The Physic" *[sk]*

- *Grimoire*, no. 2 (1982) [as "Excerpt from *Dreams of the Zodiac*," as by Louis Miguel Riaz]
- *Noctuary* (1994)

"Postscript" *[sk] [collected in "Paradoxes from Hell," op. cit.]*

- *Grimoire*, no. 4 (1983) [under the pseudonym Charles Miguel Riaz]

"Prehistoric Horror" *[see "Primordial Loathing"]*

"The Premature Death of H. P. Lovecraft, Oldest Man in New England" *[sk]*

- *Fantasy & Terror*, no. 5 (1985) [part of "Selections of Lovecraft"]
- *Crypt of Cthulhu*, 9 no. 1, whole no. 68 (Hallowmas 1989)[part of "selections of Lovecraft"]
- *The Agonizing Resurrection of Victor Frankenstein & Other Gothic Tales* (1997)

"Primordial Loathing" *[sk]*

- *Tiamet*, no 5 (June/July 1991) [as "Prehistoric Horror"]
- *Crypt of Cthulhu*, 9 no. 1, whole no. 68 (Hallowmas 1989)[as "Prehistoric Horror," part of "Studies in Horror"]
- *Noctuary* (1994)

"The Prodigy of Dreams"

- David D. Dayo, Jr. (ed). *All the Devils Are Here* (1986)
- *Crypt of Cthulhu*, 9 no. 1, whole no. 68 (Hallowmas 1989)
- *Noctuary* (1994)
- *The Nightmare Factory* (1996)

"Professor Nobody's Little Lectures on Supernatural Horror"
- *Songs of a Dead Dreamer* (1985)
- *Songs of a Dead Dreamer* (revised, 1989)

"Puppet Horror" *[see "The Puppet Masters"]*

"The Puppet Masters" *[sk]*
- *Crypt of Cthulhu*, 9 no. 1, whole no. 68 (Hallowmas 1989) [as "Puppet Horror," part of "Studies in Horror"]
- *Noctuary* (1994)

"The Real Wolf"
- *Nocturne*, no. 1 (1988)
- *Chills*, no. 5 (Spring 1991)
- Dziemianowicz (et al, eds). *100 Creepy Little Creature Stories* (1994)

"The Red Tower"
- *The Nightmare Factory* (1996)
- *Teatro Grotesco* (forthcoming)

"Salvation by Doom" *[sk]*
- *Fantasy & Terror*, no. 8 (1986) [as "Gothic Horror"]
- *Crypt of Cthulhu*, 9 no. 1, whole no. 68 (Hallowmas 1989) [as "Gothic Horror," part of "Studies in Horror"]
- *Noctuary* (1994)

"Sardonic Mundane" *[sk] [as by Louis Miguel Riaz]*
- *Grimoire*, no. 2 (1982)

"The Scream: From 1800 to the Present" *[sk]*
- *Fantasy & Terror*, no. 7 (1985)
- *The Agonizing Resurrection of Victor Frankenstein & Other Gothic Tales* (1997)

"The Sect of the Idiot"
- *Crypt of Cthulhu*, 7 no. 6, whole no. 56 (Roodmass 1988)
- *Songs of a Dead Dreamer* (revised, 1989)
- Robert M. Price (ed.). *The Azathoth Cycle* (1995)
- *The Nightmare Factory* (1996)
- "A Selection of Poe" ["The Transparent Alias of William Wilson,

Sportsman and Scoundrel"; "The Worthy Inmate of the Will of the Lady Ligeia"; and "The Interminable Residence of the Friends of the House of Usher"; see under individual titles.]

"Selections of Lovecraft" *["The Fabulous Alienation of the Outsider, Being of No Fixed Abode"; "The Blasphemous Enlightenment of Prof. Francis Wayland Thurston of Boston, Providence, and the Human Race"; "The Premature Death of H. P. Lovecraft, Oldest Man in New England"; see under individual titles]*

"Severini"

- *The Nightmare Factory* (1996)
- *Teatro Grotesco* (forthcoming)

"The Shadow, The Darkness"

- Sarrantonio, Al (ed). *999* (1999)
- *Teatro Grotesco* (forthcoming)

"The Shadow at the Bottom of the World"

- *Fear*, no. 16 (April 1990)
- *Grimscribe* (1991)
- *DAC News* (October 1994)
- *The Nightmare Factory* (1996)
- Jim Turner (ed.). *Eternal Lovecraft* (1998)

"Sideshow and Other Stories"

- *Sideshow and Other Stories* (forthcoming, planned late 2002)
- *Teatro Grotesco* (forthcoming)

"A Soft Voice Whispers Nothing"

- *In a Foreign Town, In a Foreign Land* (1997)
- *Weird Tales*, v. 55 no. 4; whole no. 316 (Summer 1999)
- *Teatro Grotesco* (forthcoming)

"Some Things They Will Never Tell You" *[verse]*

- *Some Things They Will Never Tell You* (forthcoming)

"The Spectacles in the Drawer"

- *Etchings & Odysseys*, no. 10 (1987)
- *Tales of Lovecraftian Horror*, no. 2 (June 1988)
- *Fantasy Tales*, 2 no. 3, whole no. 6 (Spring 1991)
- *Grimscribe* (1991)
- Stephen Jones and David Sutton (eds.). *The Giant Book of Fantasy Tales* (1996)
- *The Nightmare Factory* (1996)

"The Spectral Estate" *[sk]*

- *Crypt of Cthulhu*, 9 no. 1, whole no. 68 (Hallowmas 1989) [as "Spectral Horror," part of "Studies in Horror"]
- *Noctuary* (1994)

"Spectral Horror" *[see "The Spectral Estate"]*

"The Strange Design of Master Rignolo"

- *Grue*, no. 10 (Fall 1989)
- Stephen Jones and Ramsey Campbell (eds). *Best New Horror* (1990)
- *Noctuary* (1994)
- *The Nightmare Factory* (1996)

"The Striken Philosopher" *[sk] [collected in "Paradoxes from Hell," op. cit.]*

- *Grimoire*, no. 4 (1983) [under the pseudonym Charles Miguel Riaz]

"Studies in Horror" *[series of sketches, fourteen pieces, see under each individual title: "Transcendent Horror"; "Gothic Horror"; "Exotic Horror"; "Spectral Horror"; "Unreal Horror"; "Demonic Horror"; "Macabre Horror"; "Puppet Horror"; "Prehistoric Horror"; "Nameless Horror"; "Nightmare Horror"; "Occult Horror"; "Dreamworld Horror"; "Nihilistic Horror"]*

- *Crypt of Cthulhu*, 9 no. 1, whole no. 68 (Hallowmas 1989)

"The Superb Companion of Andre de V., Anti-Pygmalion" *[sk]*

- *Fantasy & Terror*, no. 7 (1985)
- *The Agonizing Resurrection of Victor Frankenstein & Other Gothic Tales* (1997)

"Tales of the New Dream" *[sk] [see "Ghost Stories for the Dead"]*

"Teatro Grottesco"

- *The Nightmare Factory* (1996)
- *Worlds of Fantasy & Horror*, no. 4 (Winter 1996-1997)
- Ellen Datlow and Terri Windling (eds), *The Years Best Fantasy and Horror: Tenth Annual Collection* (1997)
- *Teatro Grotesco* (forthcoming)

"Ten Steps to Thin Mountain"

- *Crypt of Cthulhu*, 9 no. 1, whole no. 68 (Hallowmas 1989)

"This Degenerate Little Town" *[verse]*

- *This Degenerate Little Town* (2001)
- *Teatro Grotesco* (forthcoming)

"Three Scientists" *["One Thousand Painful Variations Performed upon Divers Creatures Undergoing the Treatment of Dr. Moreau, Hu-*

manist"; "The Excruciating Final Days of Dr. Henry Jekyll, Englishman"; and "The Agonizing Resurrection of Victor Frankenstein, Citizen of Geneva," see under individual titles]

"To Conceive of Another World" *[sk] [see "Invocation to the Void"]*

"Transcendental Horror" *[see "The Master's Eyes Shining with Secrets"]*

"The Transparent Alias of William Wilson, Sportsman and Scoundrel" *[sk]*

- *Fantasy & Terror*, no. 6 (1985) [part of "A Selection of Poe"]
- *The Agonizing Resurrection of Victor Frankenstein & Other Gothic Tales* (1997)

"The Troubles of Dr. Thoss"

- *Songs of a Dead Dreamer* (1985)
- *Songs of a Dead Dreamer* (revised, 1989)
- *The Nightmare Factory* (1996)

"The Tsalal"

- *Noctuary* (1994)
- Stephen Jones and Ramsey Campbell (eds.). *The Best New Horror, v. 5* (1994)
- *The Nightmare Factory* (1996)

"Two Immortals" *["The Heart of Count Dracula, Descendent of Attila, Scourge of God"; and "The Insufferable Salvation of Lawrence Talbot the Wolfman"; see under individual titles]*

"The Unbearable Rebirth of the Phantom of the Wax Museum" *[sk]*

- *Songs of a Dead Dreamer* (1985) [under "Leading Men"]
- *The Agonizing Resurrection of Victor Frankenstein & Other Gothic Tales* (1997)

"The Unfamiliar" *[sk]*

- *Fantasy & Terror*, no. 8 (1986) [as "Exotic Horror"]
- *Crypt of Cthulhu*, 9 no. 1, whole no. 68 (Hallowmas 1989) [as "Exotic Horror," part of "Studies in Horror"]
- *Noctuary* (1994)

"The Unnatural Persecution, by a Vampire, of Mr. Jacob J." *[sk]*

- *Fantasy & Terror*, no. 7 (1985)
- *The Agonizing Resurrection of Victor Frankenstein & Other Gothic Tales* (1997)
- "Unreal Horror" [see "New Faces in the City"]

"Vastarien"

- *Crypt of Cthulhu*, 6 no. 6, whole no. 48 (St. John's Eve 1987)
- *Songs of a Dead Dreamer* (revised, 1989)
- *The Nightmare Factory* (1996)
- Robert M. Price (ed). *The New Lovecraft Circle* (1996)

"The Voice in the Bones"

- *Crypt of Cthulhu*, No. 65 (St. John's Eve 1989)
- *Noctuary* (1994)
- *The Nightmare Factory* (1996)

"What Becomes of the Body" *[verse, one of "Three Things They Will Never Tell You"]*

- [posted at The Art of Grimscribe]
- *What Becomes of the Body* (forthcoming)

"What Happens to Faces" [verse, one of "Three Things They Will Never Tell You"]

- [posted at The Art of Grimscribe]

***What Happens to Faces** (forthcoming)*

- "What Good Is Your Head" [verse, one of "Three Things They Will Never Tell You"]
- *What Good Is Your Head* (2002)
- [posted at The Art of Grimscribe]

"When You Hear the Singing, You Will Know It Is Time"

- *In a Foreign Town, In a Foreign Land* (1997)
- *Teatro Grotesco* (forthcoming)

"The Worthy Inmate of the Will of the Lady Ligeia" *[sk]*

- *Fantasy & Terror*, no. 6 (1985)
- [part of "A Selection of Poe"]
- *The Agonizing Resurrection of Victor Frankenstein & Other Gothic Tales* (1997)

OTHER NONFICTION:

[one paragraph of comments].

- Contemporary Literary Criticism, volume 44 (1987)

"The Consolations of Horror" *[essay]*

- *Horror Magazine*, no. 13 (1982)
- *Dark Horizons*, no. 27 (1984)
- *Crypt of Cthulhu*, 9 no. 1, whole no. 68 (Hallowmas 1989)

- *The Nightmare Factory* (1996) [as "Introduction"]

"The Dark Beauty of Unheard of Horrors" *[essay]*

- *Tekeli-li!*, no. 4 (Winter/Spring 1992)
- Stephen Mark Rainey (ed.). *Song of Cthulhu* (2001)

"In the Night, In the Dark: A Note on the Appreciation of Weird Fiction" *[essay]*

- *Necrofile*, No. 1 (Summer 1991) [as "Platitudes and Pontifications for the Appreciation of Weird Fiction"]
- *Noctuary* (1994)

"Jessica Amanda Salmonson: Heromaker" *[essay]*

- John C. Pelan (ed). *Axolotl Special Number One* (1989)

"Nestled in Dread: The Art of Harry Morris" [A review of *Scenes from Maldoror* by Harry O. Morris]

- *Grimoire*, no. 5 (1983)

"Platitudes and Pontifications for the Appreciation of Weird Fiction" *[see "In the Night, In the Dark"]*

"Read This" *[reading notes]*

- *The New York Review of Science Fiction*, no. 40 (December 1991)

"A Thomas Ligotti Bibliography" *[bibliography]*

- *Dagon*, no. 22/23 (September-December 1988)

"Thoughts Concerning a Decadent Universe" *[afterword]*

- David Park Barnitz, *The Book of Jade* (1998) [Limited to 300 numbered copies.]

"We Can Hide from Horror Only in the Heart of Horror" *[notes and aphorisms]*

- *Das Schwarze Geheimnis*, no. 1 (1994)
- [posted at The Art of Grimscribe]

INTERVIEWS:

Angerhuber, E. M., and Thomas Wagner. "Disillusionment Can Be Glamorous: An Interview with Thomas Ligotti," posted at *The Art of Grimscribe (*Jan. 2001).

Bee, Robert. "An Interview with Thomas Ligotti," *Spicy Green Iguana* [small press webzine], September 1999. Also posted at *Thomas Ligotti Online* (Feb 2000).

Bryant, Ed (and others). "Transcript of Chat with Thomas Ligotti on December 3, 1998," posted at the online magazine *Event Horizon* (Dec. 1998).

Dziemianowicz, Stefan. "The Tom Ligotti Interview," *Tekeli-li!*, no. 4 (Winter/Spring 1992).

Dziemianowicz, Stefan and Michael Morrison. "The Language of Dread: An Interview with Thomas Ligotti," *Science Fiction and Fantasy Book Review Annual* (1991).

Ford, Carl T. "Notes on the Writing of Horror: An Interview with Thomas Ligotti," *Dagon*, no. 22/23 (Sept.-Dec. 1988).

Friley, Mathew, with Neil Sceeny. "Grimscribe: Thomas Ligotti," *Immerse*, no. 2 (1997).

Griffin, David. "Interview with Thomas Ligotti," *Carnage Hall*, no. 3 (1992).

Paul, R.F. and Keith Schurholz. "Triangulating the Daemon," *Esoterra*, no. 8 (Winter/Spring 1999). Also posted at *Thomas Ligotti Online* (Feb 2000).

Potter, Gary D. "A Conversation with Thomas Ligotti," *The Point Beyond* (1992) [An addendum to a bookseller's catalog.]

Ramsey, Shawn. "A Graveside Chat: Interview with Thomas Ligotti," *Deathrealm*, no. 8 (Spring 1989).

Schweitzer, Darrell. "Weird Tales Talks with Thomas Ligotti," *Weird Tales*, whole no. 303 (Winter 1991-1992)

————. "A Thomas Ligotti Interview," in *Speaking of Horror*, by Darrell Schweitzer (1994) [basically a reprint of the *Weird Tales* interview].

Tibet, David. "Interview with Thomas Ligotti," *AKLO: A Volume of the Fantastic*, edited by Mark Valentine, Roger Dobson and R. B. Russell (Horam, East Sussex, and Oxford: Tartarus Press / Caermaen Books, 1998).

[Wiloch, Thomas.] "An Interview with Louis Miguel Riaz" [Ligotti as interviewee].

Grimoire, no. 2 (1982).

Winter-Damon, T. "Horror Talks with Thomas Ligotti," *Horror*, no. 3-4 (October 1994).

MISCELLANEOUS:

Ligotti can be heard reading from "Les Fleurs" in the CD by Current 93, *All the Pretty Horses* (1996).

Ligotti was contributing editor to *Grimoire*, 1982-1985.

BOOKS WITH BLURBS BY LIGOTTI:

Angerhuber, Eddie M. *Nocturnal Products* (2002).

Cardin, Matt. *Divinations from the Deep* (2003).

Cisco, Michael. *The Divinity Student* (1999).

Ford, John B. *Dark Shadows on the Moon* (2001).

Ford, John B. *Tales of Devilry and Doom* (2001).

Wiloch, Thomas. *Mr. Templeton's Toyshop: Prose Poems & Short Fiction* (1995).

CONTRIBUTORS

Douglas Anderson is a renowned Tolkien scholar whose expertise in the complicated textual history and evolution of both *The Hobbit* and *The Lord of the Rings* has led to the inclusion of his essays on these topics in most editions of those works published in English since 1987. He collaborated with Wayne G. Hammond on *J. R. R. Tolkien: A Descriptive Bibliography*. With an expertise in the history of fantasy literature, he was instrumental in reintroducing the world to E. A. Wyke-Smith's *The Marvellous Land of Snergs*, a children's fantasy that Tolkien cited as an influence on *The Hobbit*, and to such neglected writers as Kenneth Morris, Clemence Housman, and Leonard Cline. Anderson lives in southwestern Michigan.

E.M. Angerhuber (born, 1965) is a German weird fiction writer (4 German story collections and a novel published so far). Her first English book *Nocturnal Products* was published in May 2002 by Rainfall Books/GB. She does translations of works by Anglo-American writers, such as Thomas Ligotti, Ramsey Campbell, Robert Bloch, Terry Lamsley, Matt Cardin, John B. Ford and others for German publishers. She also runs the German Ligotti website "The Art of GrimScribe" (www.ligotti.de.vu) with news, bibliographies, interviews, and essays on Thomas Ligotti and a number of superb stories and poetry by Ligotti and other authors.

William Burns, in one persona, may well be a mild-mannered graduate student in Connecticut. Then again, the following may be true, that he "was born on November 11, 1972 in Cincinatti, Ohio. He served six years at Terminal Island Prison in San Pedro, California. He has a one inch scar over his left eye and woman's head tattoos on each forearm. He has one son named Valentine, presently living in Wisconsin. Correspondence c/o California State Prison, Corcoran, California."

Matt Cardin is the author of *Divinations fo the Deep*, a collection of spiritual horror stories from Ash-Tree Press. His stories and essays have appeared in *The Childen of Cthulhu, The HWA Presents: Dark Arts, The Best of Horrorfind 2, Penny Dreadful,* and elsewhere. In 2001 his academic essay "'Those Sorrows Which Are Sent to Wean Us from the Earth': The Failed Quest for Enlightenment in Mary Shelley's *Frankenstein*" was nominated for a Pushcart Prize. Matt resides in southwest Missouri with his wife and stepson, where he works as a high school English teacher and has been pursuing a graduate degree in religious studies for far too long.

Stefan Dziemianowicz has co-edited more than 30 anthologies of horror, fantasy, crime, and science fiction and collections of stories by Louisa May Alcott, Andrew Caldecott, Charles Dickens, W.C. Morrow, and Bram Stoker. The former editor of *Necrofile: The Review of Horror Fiction,* his reviews and critical writing have appeared in the *Washington Post, Publishers Weekly,* and *The Magazine of Fantasy and Science Fiction.* He is also the author of *Bloody Mary and Other Tales for a Dark Night.*

Ben P. Indick has appeared in all of Darrell Schweitzer's critical anthologies over the years and is determined to keep his record unbroken. He is a playwright, publisher of the fanzine *Ibid,* and author of *The Drama of Ray Bradbury,* critical study.

S.T. Joshi a.k.a. "the indefatigable Joshi" has done everything for H.P. Lovecraft short of creating him, by thought, out of nothing. He has written much of the standard critical literature, including *A Subtler Magick* and *H.P. Lovecraft: Decline of the West,* not to mention the definitive biography, *H.P.Lovecraft: a Life.* He has also established the standard texts in the revised Arkham House editions of Lovecraft's work, edited his collected poems and *Miscellaneous Writings,* compiled the standard bibliography, edited the leading Lovecraftian journal, *Lovecraft Studies* (in addition to its companion, *Studies in Weird Fiction*), edited *H.P. Lovecraft: Four Decades of Criticism,* and shown a wider range of critical interest with a book about Lord Dunsany and two classic studies, *The Weird Tale* and *The Modern Weird Tale.* He has also been a columnist for *Weird Tales* magazine.

Thomas Ligotti is the subject of this book.

Robert M. Price is the founder of Cryptic Publications, and long-time editor of *Crypt of Cthulhu* magazine, a journal which devoted a special issue to Thomas Ligotti. Price has also edited numerous Cthulhuoid anthologies for Fedogan and Bremer and Chaosium. He was once a mild-mannered, orthodox clergyman, but has since founded a group called Heretics Anonymous and shown his true colors delivering memorable sermons before the assembled multitudes at Cthulhu prayer breakfasts.

Darrell Schweitzer is the author of about 250 published weird/horror stories, many of which are included in his seven (so far) collections, of which some of the more recent or notable are *Transients and Other Disquieting Stories, Refugees from an Imaginary Country, Nightscapes,* and *The Great World and the Small.* His three novels are *The White Isle, The Shattered Goddess,* and *The Mask of the Sorcerer.* He has written much scholarly or critical non-fiction, including books about H.P. Lovecraft and Lord Dunsany, and edited other critical symposia like the one you're holding, including, *Discovering H.P. Lovecraft, Discovering Classic Horror Fiction, Discovering Classic Fantasy, Discovering Modern Horror Fiction* (2 vols) and *Exploring Fantasy Worlds.* He also edited the Thomas Ligotti issue of *Weird Tales* and is still co-editor of that magazine.

David Tibet is an artist, musician, and publisher. He has worked with his musical project, Hallucinatory Patripassionist rock group Current Ninety Three, since 1984; and has collaborated with many other musicians, such as Tiny Tim, Nurse With Wound, and Shirley Collins. His paintings have been exhibited in London, and have been sold all over the world. He has published the work of many authors, including Thomas Ligotti, as well as his own writings, through his Durtro and Ghost Story Press imprints. Forty-two years old, he lives in London with his wife and seven cats, where he collects paintings by Louis Wain, the work of Count Stenbock, and hoards information pertaining to the rise of Antichrist and the Apocalypse.

Jason Van Hollander (cover artist) has collaborated with Thomas Ligotti on a series of limited-edition, fine art prints. (The cover of this book illustrates "My Case for Rebributive Action" and is the first print in this series.) These colorful, gallery-quality prints are numbered, hand signed, and include a *remarque* (personal drawing) by author and artist. A signed and numbered certificate of authenticity is also included. For order details and a .pdf (electronic Adobe portable document format) catalog of other horrific fine-art collectibles, send an email to: magicpenjvh@msn.com.

Thomas Wagner, born in 1964, lives in Berlin, Germany. He writes weird fiction, reviews and essays and is an expert for European Horror cinema. His short stories and essays have been published in various German magazines and anthologies so far. He also works as a musician with his Industrial project *das pst* and has produced several audiobook CDs (eg Eddie M. Angerhuber and Thomas Ligotti).

INDEX

.